LÖWENBRAU
LÖWENBRAU
Lindner
-LINDNER-

Oktoberfest Insider Guide

Sabine Käfer

teNeues

Imprint

Editor: Sabine Käfer
Editorial coordination: Kristina Krüger, teNeues Verlag
Photos: © Münchenfoto Heinz Gebhardt (pp 3; 4; 6 photo left; 7 photo left; 10–15; 32 photo right; 43; 47; 53–59; 61–65; 67; 69; 71–84; 86–87; 89; 94–96; 99; 102–104; 108; 112 photo center; 113 photos center right, bottom; 115 photos top, center left, center right; 118–119; 120 photos day 1 top, day 2; 121 photos day 6, day 9, day 16; 122–123; 136); © Sabine Brauer Photos (pp 6 photo right; 7 photo right; 8–9; 22–23; 24 photo center; 25–31; 32 photo center; 33–38; 40 photo center; 41 photos top, bottom; 42; 44 photos center, bottom; 45 photos top, center right; 46 photo top; 48–49; 66; 68; 85; 98; 112 photos top, bottom; 113 photos top, center left; 114 photos top, center left, center right; 115 photo bottom; 120 photos day 1 bottom, day 3; 121 photo day 11; 127 photo left); © Sabine Käfer (pp 24 photos left, right; 39; 41 photo center; 100–101; 106; 121 photo day 4); © oktoberfest-tv.de (pp 32 photo left; 91–93; 110–111; 114 photo bottom); © Armin Schneider (p 46 photo center right); © www.studio-weissbacher.com (p 46 photo center left); © Michaela Klein (p 46 photo bottom); © Georg Hümpfner (p 70); © Gudrun Muschalla (p 130 photo right)
Courtesy by Regine Sixt (p 40 photo top); Lodenfrey Menswear GmbH Garching (pp 40 photo bottom; 44 photo top); Trachtenmoden Angermaier, München (p 45 photo center left); www.halfs.de (p 45 photo bottom); Hippodrom (p 52); Hofbräu-Festzelt (p 60); Münchner Knödelei (p 90); Lenbach (p 126); 8 Seasons (p 127 photo right); Milch und Bar, Veranstaltungs- und BetriebsGmbH (128 photo left); Hotel Opéra (128 photo right); Hotel Bayerischer Hof (p 129 photo left); Cafe Roma (p 129 photo right); Glockenspiel (p 130 photo left); Schumanns Tagesbar GmbH (p 131 photo left); Feinkost Käfer GmbH, München (p 131 photo right)
Drawings: Dietrun Schwarze (pp. 16–17, 19, 21, 88)
Texts: Sabine Käfer
Coauthor: Dagmar von Taube
Layout: Robert Kuhlendahl, teNeues Verlag
Production by Sandra Jansen, teNeues Verlag
Color separation by Medienteam-Vreden, Germany
Maps: M. Ramachantira, teNeues Verlag
English Translation: Jon Smale, Werkstatt München · Buchproduktion
Copyediting of the English translation by AllGerman Translations, London

Published by teNeues Publishing Group

teNeues Publishing Company
16 West 22nd Street, New York, NY 10010, USA
Tel.: 001-212-627-9090, Fax: 001-212-627-9511

teNeues Book Division
Kaistraße 18, 40221 Düsseldorf, Germany
Tel.: 0049-(0)211-994597-0, Fax: 0049-(0)211-994597-40

teNeues Publishing UK Ltd.
P.O. Box 402, West Byfleet, KT14 7ZF, Great Britain
Tel.: 0044-1932-403509, Fax: 0044-1932-403514

teNeues France S.A.R.L.
4, rue de Valence, 75005 Paris, France
Tel.: 0033-1-55766205, Fax: 0033-1-55766419

www.teneues.com

ISBN: 3-8327-9064-0

Printed in Germany

Bibliographic information published by Die Deutsche Bibliothek.
Die Deutsche Bilbiothek lists this publication in the Deutsche Nationalbibliografie;
detailed bibliographic data is available in the Internet at http://dnb.ddb.de.

Inhaltsverzeichnis

Contents

Wenn das Wiesnfieber ausbricht

Es packt mich jedes Jahr, wenn die ersten Bäume anfangen, sich zu verfärben, und die Luft wieder klarer wird. Morgens duften keine Semmeln aus dem Frühstückskorb, sondern warme Brezn. Und im Kleiderschrank warten statt der ausgedienten Sommerkleider meine bunte Dirndl darauf, endlich wieder ausgeführt zu werden. Auf dem Herd kocht dann wieder, wie jedes Jahr um diese Zeit, meine frische Hühnerbrühe – mein mitternächtlicher Krafttrunk, eine Art Betthupferl, der mich fit halten soll. Und dann kann der Wiesnmarathon, mein geliebtes Oktoberfest, beginnen.

Ich bin in Bayern groß geworden. Hier, in München, habe ich studiert. Hier war ich auch verheiratet – mit einem Wiesn-Wirt! Hier bin ich fest verwurzelt. Ich liebe unser schönes Bayern. Sie wissen schon, das ist dieses Land unterhalb des Weißwurstäquators. Alles, was darüber liegt, nennen wir Preußisches „Ausland". Sind eben ein stolzes Völkchen, wir Bayern. Stolz auf unsere eigene Sprache, unser eigenes Bier und unser eigenes Fest. Das Oktoberfest.

Ich war 16 und noch eine „Wiesn-Jungfrau", als ich an meinem ersten Bierkrug genippt habe. Was für ein bitteres Gebräu, so dachte ich damals nur.

Heute, 18 Jahre und viele Erfahrungen als Wiesn-Gängerin, als Wiesn-Reporterin und eben als Wiesn-Wirtin später, weiß ich längst: dieses Bierfest ist eine Institution des Herzens. Das Oktoberfest ist nämlich nicht nur das größte, sondern für mich und jährlich sechs Millionen andere Besucher aus allen Ecken der Erde auch das schönste Volksfest der Welt.

Gefeiert wird jedes Jahr volle 16 Tage durch. Dann bricht in ganz München und Umgebung die Bier-Euphorie aus: lacht, trinkt und umarmt sich eine ganze Stadt – ach, was sag ich, ein ganzes Land. Dann regiert in Bayern nicht mehr schwarz, sondern Gold, flüssiges Gold: das Paulaner, das Augustiner, das Löwenbräu, das Hacker-Pschorr, das Spaten-Franziskaner, das Hofbräu. Unser bestes Bier!

When the festive fever breaks out

Each year when the first leaves begin to change colour and the air becomes clearer I get this feeling. In the mornings I smell the fresh aroma of warm pretzels, rather than the usual rolls, sitting in the breadbasket and in the wardrobe colourful 'dirndls', rather than well-worn summer clothes wait to be taken out. Like every year around this time my fresh chicken broth is once again simmering on the stove–my midnight power drink, a kind of nightcap, intended to keep me fit. Everything is ready. Let the festivities, let my beloved Oktoberfest, begin.

I grew up in Bavaria, studied here in Munich, and here I was married–to the owner of a beer tent at the Oktoberfest! Here are my roots. I simply love our beautiful region. As you probably know, Bavaria is the country south of the so-called 'white veal sausage line'. Everything beyond that border is just the 'foreign land' of Northern Germany and Prussia. We Bavarians are a proud people, proud of our own language, our own beer, and our own festival ... the Oktoberfest.

I was 16 and still an 'Oktoberfest virgin' when I had my first sip from a beer mug at the 'Wiesn'. What a bitter concoction! That was all I thought at the time.

Today, eighteen years and many experiences as visitor, as special correspondent and even as manageress of a beer tent later, I now know for sure: this beer festival is an institution for and of the heart. The Oktoberfest is not only the biggest, but for me and six million visitors every year from all corners of the planet it is also the most wonderful beer festival and funfair in the world.

Each year celebrations last for sixteen whole days. All over Munich and its surrounding areas there is a veritable outbreak of beer euphoria: in the whole of the city people laugh, drink and fall into each others arms. What am I saying? Not only in Munich, in the whole country! Bavaria is then no longer ruled by the conservative black of the government but by gold, liquid gold: Paulaner, Augustiner, Löwenbräu, Hacker-Pschorr, Spaten-Franziskaner, Hofbräu. Our finest beers!

Das Phänomen dahinter ist schnell erklärt: es geht um das kollektive Erlebnis (das schließt das Kollektiv, verkatert zu sein, natürlich mit ein). Wenn nämlich alle Menschen einer Stadt gleichzeitig mit dem Wiesnfieber infiziert sind – also der Chef und die Assistentin, der Müllmann wie der Minister – hat das etwas unheimlich Identitäts- und Gemeinschaftsstiftendes. Es verbindet. Außerdem gibt so ein proppevolles und fröhlich schunkelndes Bierzelt einem das behagliche Gefühl, wie in einem kleinen Dorf zu sein. Keiner ist allein, alle sind gleich.

Und wie es nun ganz genau bei uns zugeht, das erzählt Ihnen mein *Oktoberfest Insider Guide*. Er verrät Ihnen **die besten Tipps**: wo Sie zum Beispiel mit den echten Bayern trinken oder mit den Prominenten feiern; **die ältesten Traditionen**: wie man etwa an einer Dirndl-Schürze erkennt, ob die Trägerin verheiratet oder noch zu haben ist; **die geheimsten Taktiken**: wie Sie immer ein schönes Plätzchen finden; und **sämtliche Tricks**: wie Sie eben eine Maß bestellen, ohne sich als Tourist zu outen. Er ist ein Ratgeber rund um das Oktoberfest – ein „Must“ vor der Maß für alle Zugereisten und meine ganz persönliche Liebeserklärung.

Also, auf geht's, verehrte Herrschaften: O'zapft is! Viel Spaß auf dem schönsten Volksfest der Welt.

Ihre

This phenomenon is easily explained: it is a shared, collective experience (that includes of course a collective hangover). When all the inhabitants of a city are infected by the same Oktoberfest-fever at the same time—the boss and the assistant for instance, the dustman as well as the secretary of state—it creates a very strong feeling of identity and community. It brings people together. Besides, a beer tent brimming with happy people linking arms and enjoying the music can give you the pleasant feeling of being in a small village. No-one is alone, everybody is the same.

Exactly how things happen and what ensues is explained in this *Oktoberfest Insider Guide*. It gives to you all **the best tips**: for example where you can party with celebrities or drink with real Bavarians; **the oldest traditions**: how you can recognize by the way a 'dirndl' apron is tied whether the wearer is married or still single; **the most secret strategies**: how you can always find a nice place to sit; and **all the tricks**: how you can order beer without giving yourself away as a tourist. It is a guide for everything concerning the Oktoberfest—a 'must' before the first mug of beer for all non-native visitors and my personal declaration of love.

Well now, come on, let's go, my friends: "Let the festivities begin!" Have fun at the world's greatest 'Volksfest'.

Yours

Die Wiesn

The Oktoberfest

Einst feierte ein König ...

Angefangen hat alles 1810, genau am 12. Oktober, mit einer Hochzeit: Damals heiratete der Bayerische Kronprinz und spätere König Ludwig I. die Prinzessin Therese von Sachsen-Hildburghausen. Fünf Tage dauerte das Fest, das mit einem Pferderennen auf einer Wiese vor den Toren Münchens zelebriert wurde. Diese Wiese trägt seitdem den Namen der Prinzessin und ist unsere heutige, 31 Hektar große Theresienwiese. Und weil die Hochzeitsfeier so fröhlich und gelungen war, beschloss man, die Festivität fortan als jährliches Volksfest zu feiern. Das Oktoberfest war geboren.

Aber, wieso eigentlich Oktoberfest? Schließlich beginnt das Fest, auch die Wiesn genannt, immer schon im September. Ganz einfach: Des Wetters wegen wurde es irgendwann vorverlegt. Erst 1818 floss auf dem Oktoberfest übrigens das erste Bier, in Anton Grubers erstem Bierzelt. Wenig später erhielten dann alle Brauereien Münchens die Lizenz von König Ludwig I., ihr Bier auf der Wiesn ausschenken zu dürfen.

Daneben war die große Attraktion des Oktoberfestes die „Völkerschau". Da wurde die „aussterbende Lippennegerin" auf großen Plakaten angekündigt, der „größte Mann der Welt" oder „die drei dicksten Mädchen" – Elsa mit 380 Pfund, Elvira mit 420 und Bertha mit 450 Pfund – und sogar Westernheld Buffalo Bill aus Amerika eingeschifft. So entstand die sogenannte Schaustellerei, die noch immer in kleinen Wiesn-Attraktionen wie dem „Schichtl" weiterlebt.

Nebenbei, auch heute noch spazieren echte Bayerische Prinzen über unser Volksfest! Die tragen zwar keinen Samt mehr, aber immerhin seidene Krawatte zur Tracht – Prinz Poldi von Bayern ist so einer. Um genau zu sein, er ist der Ur-Ur-Ur-Enkel von König Ludwig I. Aber vor allem ist er eins: Ein „Wiesn-Urgestein". Er kommt seit über 40 Jahren und gehört zur Wiesn wie der Hirschknopf an den Janker. Sie können sogar mit ihm um die Wette schießen. Wo? Bei Ali und Gabi, am Schießstand gegenüber der Schützen-Festhalle, unter Ludwig Schwanthalers berühmter Statue, der „Bavaria".

A king once celebrated ...

It all began with a wedding in 1810, more precisely on October 12th. In that year the Bavarian crown prince and future King Ludwig I married Princess Therese of Saxe-Hildburghausen. The festivities lasted five days and were celebrated with a horse race on a meadow beyond Munich's city walls. Since then the meadow bears the name of said princess and is our present 75 acre Theresienwiese. As the wedding celebrations were such a joyous and successful event the city fathers decided to mark the anniversary from then on every year with a funfair. The Oktoberfest was born.

But why is it called Oktoberfest? After all the beer festival, also known as the 'Wiesn', the dialect word for 'meadow', had always started in September, and it still does. The explanation is quite simple: because of the weather the starting day was at some point moved forward. By the way the first beer was not to be served at the Oktoberfest until 1818, in Anton Gruber's first beer tent. Not too long after, all of Munich's breweries were granted a license to serve beer at the 'Wiesn' by King Ludwig I.

Alongside the beer the other great event at the Oktoberfest was a mixture between an ethnic and a freak show. The 'nearly-extinct lip-negress' was advertised on large billboards, the 'tallest man in the world' or 'the three fattest girls'—Elsa at 418 pounds, Elvira at 462 and Bertha at 495 pounds, and even the hero from the Wild West, Buffalo Bill was brought over by boat. The fairground attractions were established that way. They still live on as small 'Wiesn' shows such as the Schichtl vaudeville theatre.

By the way, even these days real Bavarian princes walk around at our 'Volksfest'! They no longer wear velvet robes, but at least a silk tie to their traditional costume—Luitpold, Prince of Bavaria, is one of them. Actually, he is the great-, great-, great-grandson of King Ludwig I. But more than anything he is certainly a 'Wiesn' original. He has been a visitor for over 40 years and belongs to the 'Wiesn' like the leather braces to the 'lederhosen'. You can even go shooting with him. Where? At Ali and Gabi's shooting gallery, opposite the Schützen-Festhalle, the shooting club's beer hall, and just below Ludwig Schwanthaler's famous statue of the goddess Bavaria.

Der bayerische Urschrei

Immer am dritten Samstag im September geht das Oktoberfest los. Und das Procedere geht so: Früh morgens um zehn treffen sich die 14 Wiesnwirte der insgesamt 14 Festzelte in der Altstadt Münchens zum „Einzug der Wiesnwirte und Brauereien“, dem Auftakt des Oktoberfestes. Hinterm Sendlinger Tor warten dann schon in Reih und Glied die mit Blumen und Bändern geschmückten Festkutschen auf ihre Wiesnbarone – gefolgt von den riesigen Prachtgespannen der Brauereien.

Punkt 10 Uhr 45 ist Abfahrt. Angeführt wird der Zug von einem Mädchen auf einem Pferd, dem „Münchner Kindl“. Es trägt die Münchner Farben schwarz und gelb und ist das Glückskind der Wiesn. Ihm folgt traditionell der Oberbürgermeister im Festwagen des Schottenhamels, der wie alle Kutschen von edlen Rössern im alten Geschirr von der Sonnenstraße über die Schwanthalerstraße, vorbei an Massen winkender Menschen, direkt auf die Wirtsbudenstraße der Theresienwiese gezogen wird.

Es ist jedes Mal ein wunderschönes Bild: Die Maßkrüge schwenkenden Kellnerinnen auf den bunten Wagen. Die vollbackigen Bläser der Festkapellen, die stolzen Wirte in ihrer Tracht. Die mitmarschierenden Schausteller und Marktkaufleute. Und über allem strahlt – meistens jedenfalls – der Himmel weiß-blau.

Wenn dann kurz vor zwölf alle Kutschen vor ihren Wiesnzelten eingetroffen sind, übernimmt Münchens Oberbürgermeister Christian Ude das Regiment. Und dann wird's spannend. Punkt zwölf nämlich macht er im Schottenhamel, dem ältesten Zelt der Wiesn, den Anstich: Das erste Fass Bier wird angezapft. Nur drei Schläge braucht er, dann ist der Zapfhahn drin. Und Ude schreit: **„Oooo'zapft is!“**, dass sein Schnurrbart zittert. Das ist dann der Startschuss fürs Oktoberfest. Der Bürgermeister trinkt den ersten Schluck. Aus der Ferne kracht es zwölf Mal, wenn die Schützen unter der Bavaria ihre Böllerschüsse feuern. Und mit dem zwölften fließt schließlich das Bier aus allen Hähnen.

The Bavarian 'primal scream'

The Oktoberfest always begins on the third Saturday in September, and the procedure is as follows: at ten in the morning the 14 managers of the 14 beer tents at the Oktoberfest, gather in the old part of Munich for the 'procession of the beer tent managers and breweries', the start of the Oktoberfest. Behind the Sendlinger Tor the festival carriages, decorated with flowers and ribbons, wait in a neat row for their 14 'Wiesn barons'–followed by the magnificent horse-drawn coaches of the breweries.

At 10:45 on the dot they start to move. The parade is lead by a girl on horseback, the 'Münchner Kindl'. She wears the municipal colours, black and yellow, and she is the lucky charm of the 'Volksfest'. Munich's Mayor traditionally follows her in the carriage of the Schottenhamel tent, that like all carriages is drawn by thoroughbreds in traditional harnesses. The procession moves from Sonnenstraße via Schwanthalerstraße, past a mass of cheering spectators, and then directly onto the so-called Wirtsbudenstraße ('beer tent lane') of the Theresienwiese.

Every time it looks like a picture postcard: The waitresses on colourful wagons waving large beer steins, the musicians of the brass bands with their round cheeks, the proud beer barons in their traditional dress, the showmen and food or souvenir sellers from the fairground attractions marching along behind. And high above the sky is bright–usually at any rate–and shows the Bavarian national colours, blue and white.

Then shortly before twelve, when all the carriages have arrived in front of their beer tents, Munich's Mayor Christian Ude takes charge of the proceedings. The tension mounts. At the stroke of twelve in the Schottenhamel tent, the oldest tent on the 'Wiesn', with brass tap and mallet in hand, he begins the tapping: The new draft from the first barrel of the Oktoberfest. He only needs three mallet strokes to drive home the brass tap. And Christian Ude, his mustache quivering as he cries out in dialect: **"Oooo'zapft is!"** (the barrel is tapped!). This is the starting signal for the Oktoberfest. The Bürgermeister drinks the first drop of beer. In the distance twelve gunshots can be heard when the men from the shooting clubs fire their gun salutes below the Bavaria statue. And on the twelfth shot the beer begins to flow in every beer tent!

Die Wiesn in Zahlen*

6 Mio. Besucher kommen ungefähr pro Jahr auf das Oktoberfest.
people more or less visit the 'Wiesn' every year.

14 große Bierzelte und **50** kleine Zelte und Bude
big beer tents and small tents and stall

5 Mio. Liter Bier werden im Schnitt getrunken.
litres of beer are drunk on average.

1 Maß sollten 1 Liter Bier sein und kosten um die 7 Euro.
(pron. 'maas', = mug of beer) should be one full litre and costs about €

700 000 Hendl werden während einer Wiesn verspeist,
roast chicken are consumed in one season,

200 000 Steckerlfische verzehrt,
smoked fish are eaten,

90 Ochsen verputzt,
oxen devoured,

20 000 Essensbestellungen pro Zelt an starken Tagen serviert.
orders for meals are taken on busy days per tent.

* alle Angaben aus dem Jahr 2004 und ohne Gewähr

The Oktoberfest in figures*

216 Schausteller (Fahrgeschäfte und Buden) gibt es auf der Wiesn.
fairground attractions (side-shows, rides, stalls and booths) take part in the 'Wiesn'.

varten auf die durstigen Gäste.
await their thirsty guests.

535 „Bierleichen" wurden von den Sanitätern versorgt,
binge drinkers are attended to by paramedics.

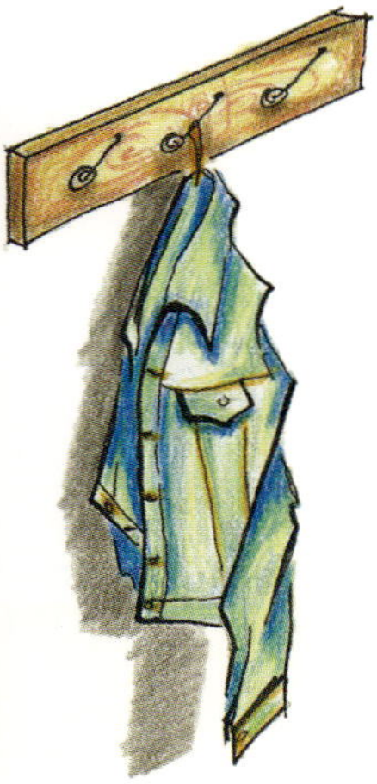

3800 Dinge als verloren gemeldet, darunter ...
items of property are reported lost, including ...

1050 Kleidungsstücke ...
articles of clothing ...

420 Schlüssel ...
sets of keys ...

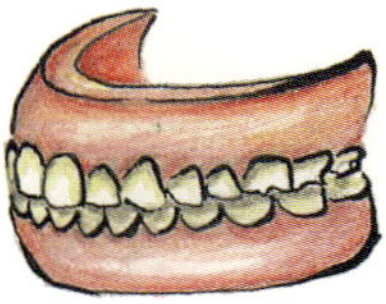

3 Gebisse.
dentures.

195 000 fast geklaute Bierkrüge wurden vom Ordnungspersonal sicher gestellt.
almost-stolen beer mugs are confiscated by security personnel.

36 000 Maßkrüge gingen dennoch beim Feiern in nur einem Zelt zu Bruch.
beer mugs still get broken in the commotion in one single tent.

*All figures date from 2004, no liability assumed.

Der Bayer an sich – sein Wesen:

Für die Bayern ist Bayern immer noch ein Königreich.

„Wer hier lebt“, sagt mein Freund und Wiesn-Wirt Wiggerl Hagn – und er muss es wissen, ist schließlich selbst Bayer mit Leib und Seele – **„ist ein liebenswert, grantelnder Sturschädel, der wenig spricht, und wenn, dann gern dabei murrt. Aber vor allem macht der Bayer eines: nämlich grundsätzlich nicht das, was man von ihm erwartet.“**

Er ist eben ein ehrsinniger Gesell. Stolz ist sein zweites Wappentier. Und Recht hat der Bayer, sein Bayern zu lieben: Das Land mit seinen Schlössern, Bergen und Seen. Und mittendrin der Bayer selbst, der alles mag, was gemütlich ist: Sein Heim, sein Weib (immer auf seiner Seite, nur daheim hat sie die Pantoffeln an!), seinen Schnupftabak, seine Ruh. Und seinen Schweinebraten natürlich, aber den nur mit Kartoffelknödel! So wie er die Weißwurst auch nur vor zwölf Uhr isst.

Ja, Essen ist für den Bayern wie Freundschaft: Eine Sache von Verlässlichkeit. Wohl darum heißt auch jeder zweite Bayer Sepp – von Joseph. Nur „Seppl“ sollten Sie den Bayern nicht nennen. Das ist ein Schimpfwort. Und schimpfen darf schließlich nur er. Drum schimpft der Bayer auch jedes Jahr auf das Oktoberfest, bevor es überhaupt begonnen hat: Zu laut! Zu voll! Zu teuer! Und wer hockt dann schließlich da, sechzehn Tage durchgehend an seinem Wiesn-Stammtisch? Der Bayer, eh klar ... ist eben herrlich liebenswert!

The Bavarian–his nature:

For Bavarians their country remains a kingdom.

“Everyone who lives here”, my friend and ‘Wiesn’ tent manager Wiggerl Hagn says–and he should know, he is a Bavarian himself, with heart and soul–, **“is amiable, grumpy, and stubborn, someone who says little, and if he does open his mouth to speak he usually grumbles a bit as well. But above all the Bavarian does one thing best: exactly the opposite of what people expect of him.”**

He has simply got his own notion of honour. Pride is the other side of his character. Bavarians are quite right that they adore their Bavaria: the country with the castles, mountains and lakes. The Bavarian himself sits right in the middle of it and likes comfortable things above all else: his house, his wife (always on his side, only at home she is the one in charge!), his snuff, his peace and quiet. He loves his ‘Schweinebraten’ (roast pork), but insists on having it served with potato dumplings! Just as he will only eat the traditional white veal sausage before lunch time.

Yes, for Bavarians food is like friendship, a matter of reliability. Perhaps that is why every second male Bavarian is called Sepp–short for Joseph. You should not really call a Bavarian ‘Seppl’ though. That is an insult, and as we all know only the Bavarian himself is allowed to swear and insult and complain. Every year he moans about the Oktoberfest before it has even started: it’s too loud, too crowded, too expensive! But, look, who’s that sitting over there? Sixteen days straight at his regular table? The Bavarian, of course, being marvellously amiable.

Die bayerische Tracht

Der Bayer zeigt gern, dass er Bayer ist. Darum trägt er seine Tracht auch stolz wie eine Uniform. Dabei hat jede Region ihre eigene Tracht (Kurzform für: „so wurde es getragen"): also die Miesbacher, die Chiemgauer etc. Die Münchner haben das sogenannte schwarze „Mieder g'wand". Diese prachtvollen Trachten sieht man allerdings nur noch selten, z.B. beim Wiesn-Trachtenumzug. Auf der Wiesn werden Dirndl und Lederhosen getragen.

So geht Sie: Tief dekolletiert lautet ihr oberstes Kleidergebot. Wem das zu nackert ist, der kann auch seine Gardinen etwas zuziehen. Gemeint ist die reich gerüschte Spitzenbluse, die zu ihrem Dirndl gehört wie die Schürze aus Baumwolle oder auch Taft. Rechts gebunden verrät sie, die Trägerin ist verheiratet, links gebunden – noch frei! Gekrönt wird ihr Outfit mit dem Kropfband, dem Trachten-Halsschmuck, sowie dem Fransentuch über den Schultern.

Und so geht Er: Zur Lederhosen mit Gürtel oder Hosenträgern trägt er das Pfordlhemd mit Monogramm. Und den Charivari, das silberne Prachtgehänge mit Münzen und Symbolen vorm Hosenlatz, das für Zunft und Reichtum steht. Wichtig auch noch: der Haferlschuh. Und der Gamsbart als Jagdtrophäe auf dem Hut aus Wildhasenhaar, sowie das Hirschfängermesser an der Lederhose.

Bavarian traditional dress

Bavarians are happy to show where they are from. That is why they wear their traditional costume like a proud uniform. Every region has its own style. Costumes from say the Miesbach region would look different to clothes from the Chiemgau region for example. The inhabitants of Munich have the so-called black 'bodice frock'. All these magnificent clothes are rarely seen nowadays, but on one occasion they are shown off: the parade in traditional dresses on the second day of the 'Wiesn'. At the Oktoberfest people usually wear 'dirndls' and 'lederhosen'.

What she wears: Whatever the dress, it must be very low cut. But if that is deemed a little too revealing the 'curtain' can be drawn. The 'curtain' in this case is a blouse made out of lace with lots of small frills. It is part of the dirndl just like the cotton or taffeta apron. Fastened to the right, the apron reveals the wearer to be married and fastened to the left means she is single. The finishing touches to her outfit are a choker and a fringed shawl over her shoulders.

What he wears: With his 'lederhosen', worn with either belt or braces, he prefers a traditional shirt, the so-called Pfordlhemd, with a monogram and a 'charivari', a silver decorative chain of coins and medallions, attached in front of the codpiece and a symbol for his guild and wealth. Also quite important are the accessories: the Alpine-style loafer, the so-called Haferlschuh, plus a hunting trophy made out of goat hair attached to a hat of wild rabbit hair and finally a single-edged hunting knife carried in one of the pockets on the side of the 'lederhosen'.

Die 8 Wiesntypen

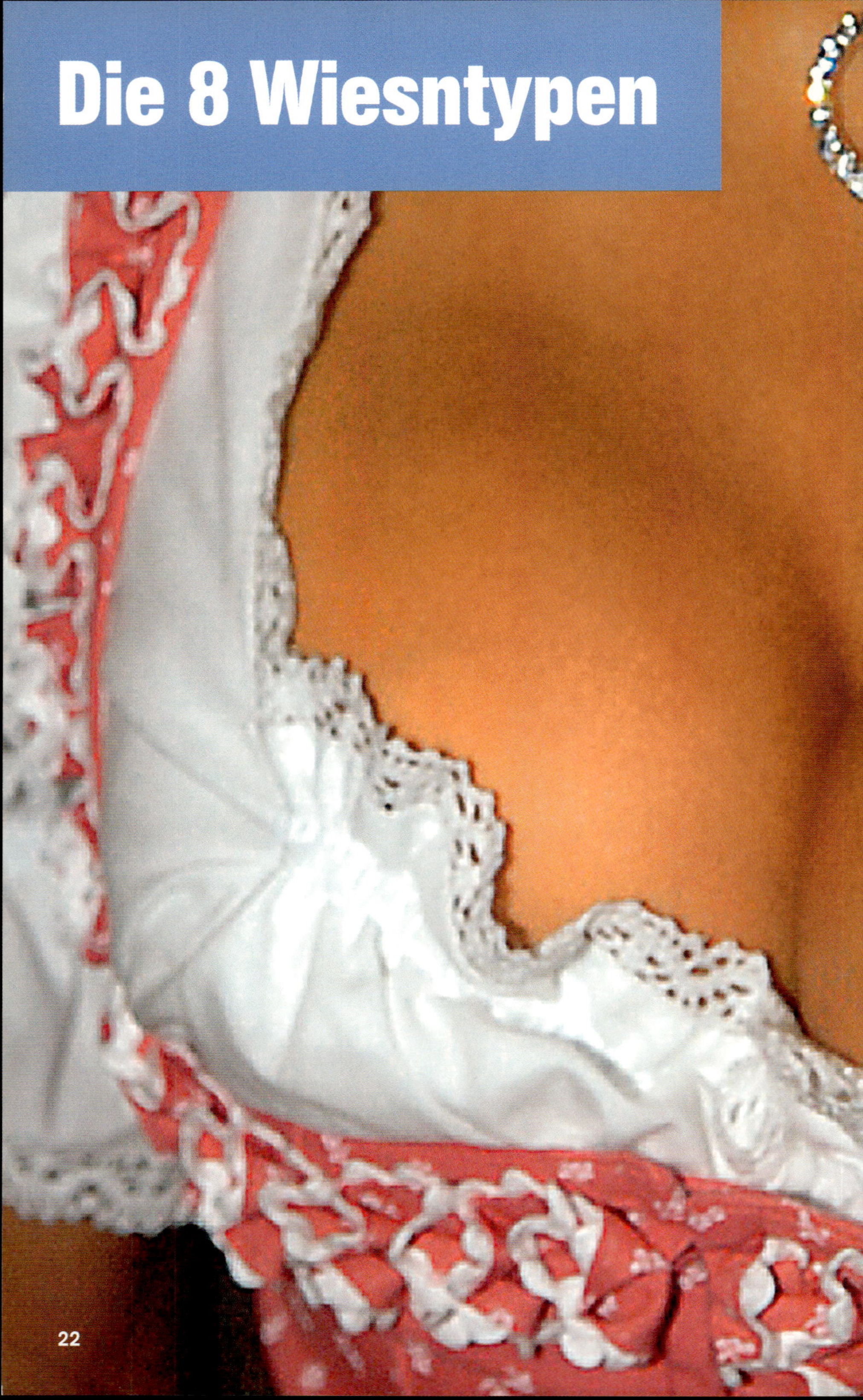

8 Types of Visitors

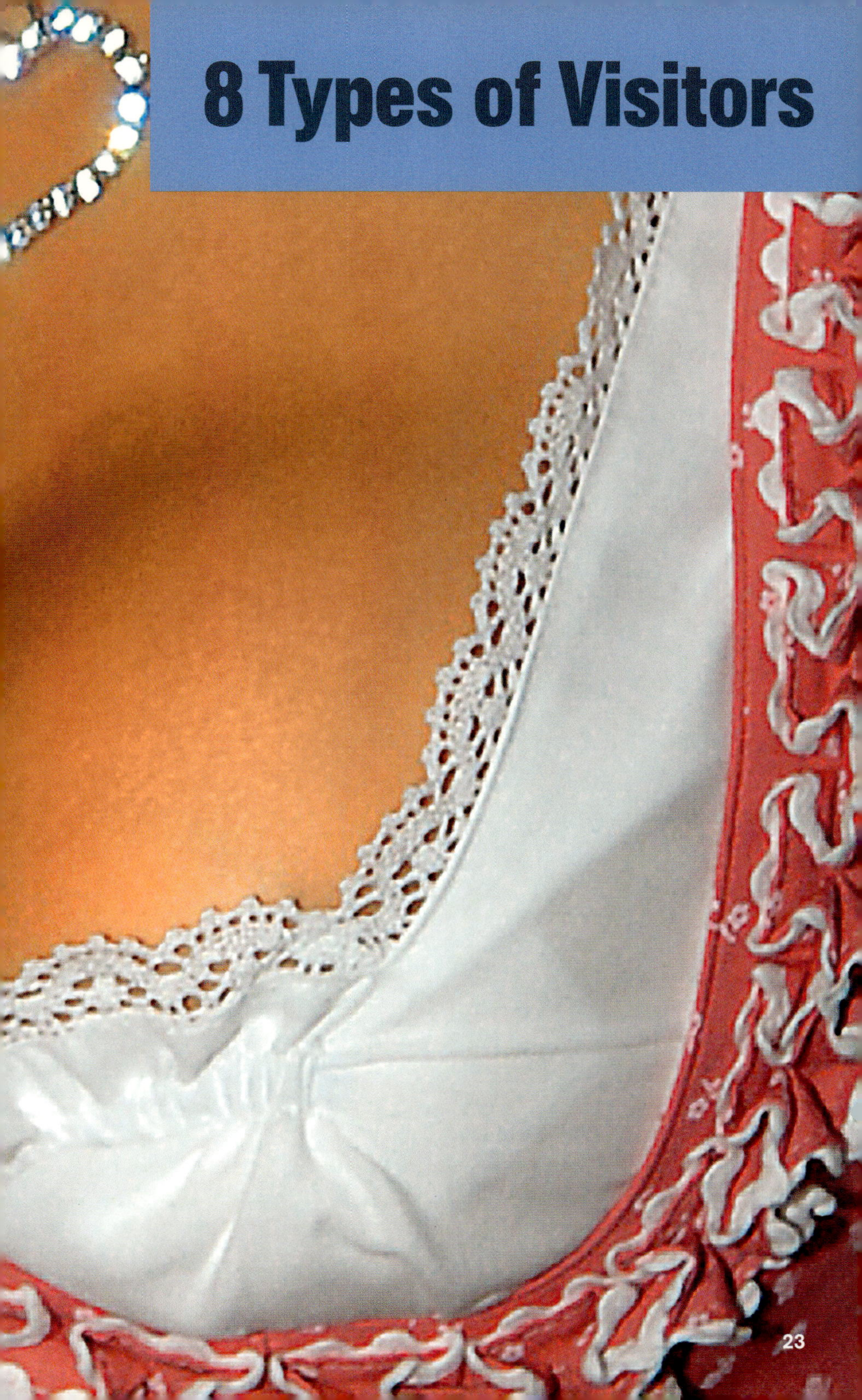

Das Münchner Original

Die einheimischen Wiesnbesucher kommen in der Woche. Denn an den überfüllten Wochenenden machen sie lieber den Zugereisten Platz. Mit lauter Fremden auf seiner Wiesn fühlt sich der Einheimische einfach nicht mehr richtig zu Hause. Genauso graust ihm beim Gedanken an den Lärm in so einem abendlichen Bierzelt. Darum kommt er, wenn überhaupt, nur mit Einladung und festem Tisch. Oder mittags, wenn es sonnig und gemütlich und die Wiesn für ihn am schönsten ist. Dann schießt der Einheimische mal eine Rose für seine Frau, derweil sie eine Tüte Mandeln isst. Danach fährt er irgendwas, danach hat er Magengrummeln, worauf sich beide in irgendein Zelt setzen. Und dort sitzen bleiben. Und Leute gucken. Und ratschen. Und ein paar Maß trinken. Spätestens jetzt würden andere die Hemmungen verlieren. Nicht so der Einheimische. Der sagt: „Grad gmütlich is“. Gegen Bier ist er quasi immun. Damit ist er aufgewachsen wie mit der Tracht. Die steht ihm wohl auch deshalb wie angegossen. Jeder Andere in Dirndl oder Lederhose wirkt schnell verkleidet. Nur die Einheimische trägt ihr Dekollete selbstverständlich vor sich her, dass Dutzend Herrennasen hineinpurzeln möchten. Während er, der Einheimische, mit seiner Krachledernen und seinem Janker mühelos jedes Casting für einen Heimatfilm gewinnen könnte.

The Native

You need to go on a weekday to find a Munich native. They tend to leave the field to ‘outsiders’ on the overcrowded weekends. With all these outsiders at his ‘Wiesn’, the native simply does not feel at home any more. He also shudders in disgust at the thought of all the noise in the beer tents in the evening. Therefore he only goes, if at all, by invitation and with a table reserved for him. Or he chooses to go at lunchtime when the weather is sunny and pleasant and for him the ‘Wiesn’ is at its best. Then the native man may win a plastic rose for his wife at the shooting gallery while she happily munches her roasted almonds. After that he will take a ride in one of the fairground attractions which in turn will upset his stomach. They will then proceed to one of the beer tents. And stay there, watching the crowd, chatting, drinking a few pints. Others would have lost their inhibitions by now. But not the native. He says to himself: “This is alright, I think ...”. He is virtually immune to the effects of beer. He grew up with it and also with his traditional dress. That is why it fits him like a glove. Everybody else wearing ‘dirndl’ or ‘lederhosen’ just looks dressed up. Only the native woman is able to wear her low-cut dirndl so naturally that dozens of men would love to take an even closer look. The native man with his original ‘lederhosen’ and traditional jacket (the so-called ‘Janker’) could easily play the starring role in any ‘Heimatfilm’, the regional version of the sentimental romance.

Der Aristokrat

Sie enden meist auf „i", die Trixi's, Maxi's, Onkel Möpi's, oder Tante Mausi's. Dabei sind ihre wahren Namen so lang wie Menükarten. Der Aristo hat eben, wie der Bayer auch, seine eigene Sprache, das sogenannte „Schlossdeutsch" (Merkmal: Langgezogene Adjektive wie „waaahnsinnig gemüüütlich", „raaasend kooomisch"; und: etwas ist „köstlich", nicht „lecker"!). Genauso hat er sein eigenes Zelt, die Schützen-Festhalle, und seinen eigenen Dress-Code, was praktisch ist, weil der Aristo so schnell zu seinem Rudel findet und somit sicher unter sich bleibt. Für die Herren gelten gedeckte Farben aus dem Jagdsport, wie tannengrüner Loden zu Jeans und Janker aus cognacfarbenem Babycord. Dazu Accessoires wie Siegelringe (der norddeutsche Aristo), Monogramme auf kleinkarierten Maßhemden oder ausgefallene Stilbrüche wie Krawatte zur Krachledernen. Nur neu darf es nicht aussehen! Getragenes sollte geerbt wirken, was nicht etwa für Verarmung steht, sondern lediglich das Traditionsbewusstsein unterstreicht. Das Kleiderdiktat für die Herzdame des Aristo lautet ebenfalls: Dezente Zurückhaltung. Außer beim Schmuck. Der darf, ob nun geerbt, nagelneu oder auch nur modisch kopiert, schon ein bisschen was hergeben. Dabei sind Bandringe meist Ausdruck für Gebärfreudigkeit und Panzerarmbänder für Hochzeiten und sonstige Vergehen angebracht.

The Aristocrat

Their names usually end in 'i', like for instance Trixi, Maxi, Uncle Möpi or Aunti Mausi whereas their real names are as long as menus. The aristocrat, just like Bavarians, has his own language: the so-called 'palace German' (characteristics: multi-syllabic adjectives that can be drawn out such as "friiightfully cheeerful", "aaawfully fuuunny"; and food, of course, is "delicious" and not just "good"). He also has his own tent, the Schützen-Festhalle (shooting club's beer hall), and his own dress code, which helps him to quickly recognise his peers and thus remain safely amongst his own. Dress-code for gentlemen: subdued colours, preferably with an association to hunting, like pine-green loden with jeans and a 'Janker' jacket in Cognac-coloured fine corduroy. Accompanied by accessories like signet rings (for the Northern German nobleman), monograms on a tailored shirt in small chequered print or unusual combinations such as ties with 'lederhosen'. But under any circumstances is it to look new. Heaven forbid! All garments should appear inherited. But this is not a sign of a decline in fortune, it only demonstrates a sense of tradition. The fashion for the gentleman's lady also prescribes: discretion and reticence. Except for the jewellery; whether inherited, brand new or just fashionable, it can and should show off. Rings are often a sign for fertility and metal bracelets suitable for marriages and other misdemeanours.

Die Offenherzigen

Die Wiesn ist zum „Anbandeln“ da. Als ob der liebe Gott bei den Offenherzigen seine Finger im Spiel gehabt hätte: Das Dekollete dieser reizvollen Geschöpfe sitzt perfekt zum Auftritt ihrer großen Wiesn-Roben, wie glitzernde Alpenröcke oder schulter- und beinfreie Couture-Dirndl zum perfekten Make-Up. Mehr Laufsteg als Wiesn eigentlich. Darum sind die Schönheiten auch nicht zum Anfassen da, sondern nur zum Gucken und Staunen.

Für die von Gottes Gnaden weniger Dekolletierten, hält die Industrie raffinierte Hilfsmittel bereit, wie den „Air-Bra“ mit aufblasbaren Luftkissen, in die je nach Situation und Anlass nachgepumpt werden kann. Kenner erledigen das mit einer dazugehörigen kleinen Pumpe, vorzugsweise in der Geisterbahn – und nicht im Bierzelt. Somit hat der Schürzenjäger die Qual der Wahl, und kann nur hoffen, dass seinem feschen Madl zuhause nicht die Luft ausgeht.

The Revealingly Open-hearted

The Oktoberfest is there to flirt. It feels like as if nature had intended to create such startling creatures as these open-hearted, revealingly dressed ladies: their cleavage sits perfectly, ready for the grand entry. To their 'Wiesn' gown belong glittery Alpine-style skirts or strapless and bare-legged, tailor-made 'dirndls' and of course perfect make-up. More fashion show than beer festival. These beauties are there to be looked at and admired but not to be touched.

For those less favoured by nature modern technology has come up with intricate solutions, such as the 'air bra' with inflatable pouches that, depending on the situation or occasion, can be filled with air. Experts take care of this with a small pump supplied together with the bra, preferably in the darkness of the ghost train–and not in the beer tent. Consequently the philanderer may be spoilt for choice and can only hope that his pretty girl does not loose her firmness as soon as they get home.

Der Preiß

Den Preußen erkennt man daran, dass er meist bayerischer ausschaut als der Bayer selbst. Ein Wiesnausflug ist für ihn ein großes emotionales Erlebnis, weil er nicht genau weiß, was ihn erwartet. Darum erkundigt er sich exakt: Was zieh' ich an, um bloß nicht aufzufallen. Und geht vor der Wiesn noch extra schnell die falschen Sachen kaufen. Aber wenigstens steht er dann in kompletter, nagelneuer, brettsteifer Vollkombi-Montur da: Von den Haferlschuhen bis zum Halstüchlein voll durchgestylt. Solchermaßen ausstaffiert fühlt sich der Preuße angenommen, wenn er über den Weißwurstäquator zu den Bayern reist. Dort zerlegt er dann sein Hendl mit Messer und Gabel, schlürft seine Weinschorle oder hält den Bierkrug am Glas, nicht wie der Wiesnprofi fest am Henkel. Vom Inhalt allerdings verträgt er wie der Bayer viel. Und „outet" sich dann richtig – durch seine Mund-Art, wenn er Glück beseelt Lieder singt wie „Geld ham'ma, Moos ham'ma, reich sam'ma, Scheich sam'ma", und der erste ist, der auf die Tische springt. Ja, er kann feiern, der Preuße. Und verliert im Rausch selten die Contenance.

The Northerner from Prussia

The 'Preiß' or Northerner from Prussia can easily be recognized because he looks more Bavarian than the Bavarians themselves. A visit to the Oktoberfest is a very emotional experience for him as he does not know exactly what to expect. He therefore tries to find out as much as he can beforehand: "What do I wear in order not to stand out?" And just before the big day he goes shopping and buys all the wrong clothes. But at least he wears the complete outfit from the tie to the loafer: brand new, colour coordinated, top to bottom and stiff as a board. Thus equipped the Northerner feels accepted by the locals when he descends across the border into Bavaria. Once there he uses knife and fork to eat his roast chicken, sips his spritzer or holds his beer mug by the shaft—unlike the 'Wiesn'-expert who uses the handle. Still, he can take a lot of the liquid content, just like Bavarians. He gives himself away though as soon as he opens his mouth and in his bliss tries to sing Bavarian songs in the original dialect. He is also the first to jump onto the tables. You have to admit he really can party, this Northerner, and in his state of intoxication rarely looses his composure.

HIPPO

Die Wiesn-Touris

Die durstige Invasion aus Japan, Australien, England, Skandinavien, Amerika, Italien ist leicht erkennbar, weil sie eine Vorliebe für alles hat, was Geräusche macht, blinkt und/oder auf den Kopf zu setzen ist: rülpsende Plüschmaßkrüge, Sepplfilz-Hüte und blinkende Teufelshörner. Damit behängen sich diese rührenden Souvenir-Jäger zumeist gleich kiloweise. Zwar tragen sie keine bayerische Tracht – brauchen sie auch nicht. Sie haben ihren eigenen Look: Jeans. Turnschuhe, Sonnenbrille, Kamera. Wenn sie dann noch ein „I mog di"-T-Shirts mit knutschenden Bayern-Löwen ergattern konnten, versetzt sie das in höchste Ekstase. Was ihre Leidenschaft zum Bier noch kräftiger unterstützt. Für Ihre erste Maß brauchen sie noch zwei Stunden und beim Hendl fragen sie nach Ketchup, fühlen sich aber schon wie echte Bayern. Treffen kann man den Wiesn-Touri entweder in allen großen Zelten, wo er gelernt hat: ab neun darf er auf die Bänke. Und die weiblichen Begleitungen heben die Pullover. Oder er schläft unter der Bavaria nach ein paar Krügen seinen Rausch aus. Darum, wegen des Open-Air-Gefühls, glaubt er auch, heiße Bayern „Freistaat".

The 'Wiesn' Tourists

The thirsty invaders from Japan, Australia, Britain, Scandinavia, America and Italy can easily be spotted. They like anything that flashes, makes a noise and/or can be worn on one's head: burping fluffy beer mugs, floppy felt hats and flashing devil's horns. These touching souvenir hunters wear these usually by the dozen. They do not dress in traditional Bavarian costume, but then again they do not have to. They have their own look: jeans, trainers, sunglasses, camera. If they then manage to acquire a T-shirt saying 'I Mog Di' (Bavarian for 'I Love You') sporting kissing lions they are in heaven, which leads to an even higher consumption of beer. For their first two pints they still take two hours and they ask for ketchup for the roast chicken, but they feel like real Bavarians. You can find 'Wiesn' tourists either in all the large beer tents (where they have found out that after nine they are allowed to dance on the benches and their female companions lift their jumpers). Or after a few pints they sleep off their inebriation below the Bavaria statue. Due to this open-air feeling they believe that that is the reason why the state of Bavaria is called the 'Free State'.

CROATIAN
DRINKING TEAM

Die jungen Wilden

Das Oktoberfest gehört gewissermaßen zu ihrer Ausbildung, bei der die, die wie eine Stadt oder ein Land (z.B. „v. Bieberstein", „v. Hohenlohe") heißen, sich in Volkstümlichkeit üben. Oder die, die auf den Namen einer Firma (z.B. „Faber-Castell") hören, ersten Kontakt zum Kunden erfahren. Und Mädels und Buben, die alle so aussehen, als wären sie gerade aus irgendwelchen Eliteinternaten oder Mädchenpensionaten ausgebüchst, sich kennen lernen können. Zum Sitzen kommt dieses fröhliche Wiesen-Völkchen kaum. Nein, wer zwischen 15 und 35 Jahre alt und wild ist, der läuft rum, um die „Area zu checken". Besonders, wenn am ersten Wiesnsamstag ein amerikanisches Juwelierhaus mit Türkiser Logofarbe zum „Wiesn-Frühstück" in die Schützen-Festhalle oder am Tag darauf das Käferzelt zum legendären „Almauftrieb" bitten: Die Mädchen posen mit adrett wippenden Pferdeschwänzchen im dottergelben Wasch-Dirndl von Mami, im Rocktäschchen das Notbesteck Lippgloss und Kaugummis. Die Jungs wie junge Landwirte in Papis Lederhose, das Bier mehr sonst wo als im Glas. So, in Tracht, feiern sie dann übrigens noch in der Disko nach der Wiesn weiter.

The Bright Young Things

In some way the Oktoberfest is part of their education. Those whose names sound like towns or counties (e.g. 'von Bieberstein' or 'von Hohenlohe') rub shoulders with the populace at the Oktoberfest. Those whose family names belong more to the company than themselves (e.g. 'Faber-Castell') experience their first contacts with clients. What's more, girls and boys who look like they have just escaped from some elite boarding or finishing school can now get to know each other. They hardly ever get to sit down for long though. Oh no, everyone between 15 and 35 and still a Bright Young Thing do their rounds to 'check out all areas'. Especially when on the first Oktoberfest Saturday a big American jeweller with a turquoise logo requests their presence at their 'Wiesn' breakfast in the Schützen-Festhalle (shooting club's beer hall) or when on the next day at the famous Käfer's delicatessen tent (Käfer's Wies'n Schänke) these young ones are shepherded to the 'Almauftrieb', one of the legendary parties: The girls pose in Mummy's canary yellow 'dirndl' with their neat pony tails bobbing up and down, in their skirt pockets emergency lip-gloss and chewing gum. The boys look like young farmers in Daddy's 'lederhosen' and get the beer more onto their clothes than into their mouths. By the way after the Oktoberfest they go clubbing, still in their traditional dress.

Die Schickerianer

Diese Fraktion aus Fußballern, Schlagersängern oder Immobilienhaien gehört zur Wiesn wie die Hefe ins Bier. Zwar gelten die Schickimickis als äußerst unkompliziert – gebt Ihnen ein Bier und ein Sonnenplätzchen und sie sind glücklich. Trotzdem haben sie neben ihrem Hendl auch ihre Extrawürste nicht ungern. So residiert z.B. Ralph Siegel in seiner Haus-Box, die er auf Lebzeiten gepachtet hat, und immer zu seinem Geburtstag wird sogar eigens ein Piano angeliefert. Und ein Fußballkaiser freut sich über persönlichen Begleitschutz, wenn er dorthin geht, wo Kaiser normalerweise allein hingehen: aufs Häusl nämlich. Weil ihm so der schnellste Weg gebahnt wird. „'Seng und g'seng werden" ist nun mal des Schickimickis Devise. Darum putzt er sich auch raus und dekoriert sich fleißig. Beliebte Outfits: Dirndl in rosa und hellblau, den Farben ferner Kindertage, sowie Landhaustrachten aus Sackleinen und Samt. Karohemden, vor allem aber Accessoires wie das zum Hemd passende Karo-Halstuch, die Ansteckrose im Knopfloch, das Einstecktüchlein, das aus dem Janker lupft und Stickereien überall dort, wo noch Stoff frei ist. Dieser Wiesn-Typ ist nie zu blass. Umso weißer ist sein Lächeln. Und wo der umschwärmte, prominente Schickimicki auf seiner Wiesn hockt, ist meist ein Regional-TV-Team nicht weit, um am nächsten Tag brühwarm den neuesten Wiesntratsch zu vermelden.

The In-crowd

This group consists of footballers, pop singers or property developers and they belong to the 'Wiesn' like yeast to beer. Although the glitterati are known to be extremely uncomplicated–give them a beer and a place in the sun and they are happy–they do like their roast chicken and also that little bit of special treatment they are so used to. Ralph Siegel, Germany's answer to Pete Waterman, for instance resides in a private box that he has rented for life, and every birthday a piano is delivered specially. The president of Bayern Munich is pleased to have brought his bodyguard who can lead the way through the crowd to the place where even famous footballers have to go on their own: the loo. That way he will take the shortest route. The In-crowd's mission statement is after all 'To see and be seen'. So they dress up. Favourite outfits are 'dirndl' in pink and baby blue, colours from the faraway days of childhood, as well as country dresses made out of hessian and velvet. Checked shirts, but most of all accessories such as the chequed scarf to match the shirt, a rose in the buttonhole, a handkerchief popping out of the jacket's top pocket and embroideries wherever there is space on the garment. This type of visitor to the 'Wiesn' can never be too pale, his smile is even whiter. Wherever celebrities can be found sitting in a tent at the Oktoberfest, a regional TV team is never far off to disseminate the latest, hot-from-the-press 'Wiesn' gossip the very next day.

Die Zwillingspaare

Auch das Paarlaufen ist ein Phänomen auf der Wiesn. Dazu gehören all jene Verliebte, Verheiratete und schon fast wie Zusammengewachsene, die nur zu zweit kommen, zu zweit sitzen und zu zweit wieder gehen. Darum sehen sich diese Paare oft auch schon so ähnlich, dass sie Geschwister sein könnten. Seit der Geburt getrennt sozusagen. Egal, wie viele Verrückte um sie herum torkeln, diese Paare fallen sich in die Arme. Und zwei Hälften werden zu einem Kreis, bei dem man nicht mehr erkennt, welcher Arm zu wem gehört. Klar, Paare gehen im Partnerlook: Das wiesenblumenbestickte Trachtenhemd für Sie gibt es auch in seiner Größe. Genauso kommen Lederhose und Haferlschuhe im Doppelpack. Viele Paare sind sich schon auf der Wiesn näher gekommen. Das geht übrigens prima beim Anstehen an den Toiletten, vorm Karussell oder im Bierzelt-Gedränge. Das Kennenlernen kann man dann jährlich mit einem Jubiläums-Hendl, z.B. am Zweier-Tisch unter der Holztreppe in Käfer's Wies'n Schänke immer wieder feiern. Die Wiesn kann auch sehr romantisch sein!

The Twins

Even synchronised walking can be a phenomenon at the Oktoberfest. To this group belong all those in love, married couples and those almost grown into one who arrive together, sit together and leave together. These couples often look so alike that they could almost be siblings—separated at birth as it were. No matter how many drunken lunatics fall about around them these couples fall only into each other's arms. Two halves create one circle where nobody can tell which arm belongs to which body anymore. Of course couples dress in the same clothes: Her traditional shirt embroidered with wild flowers is also available in his size. Similarly 'lederhosen' and Alpine-style loafers come in twos. A lot of couples got much closer at the Oktoberfest. You can give it a shot while queuing for the toilets or standing in front of the Ferris wheel or even in the throng of the beer tent. The first encounter can then be celebrated every year with an anniversary dinner of roast chicken, e.g. at a table for two under the wooden staircase in Käfer's delicatessen tent (Käfer's Wies'n Schänke). The Oktoberfest can be very romantic indeed.

VIP Wiesn-Tipps

Meine Wiesn-Freunde und ihre ganz geheimen Tipps

Celebrity Tips

My Oktoberfest colleagues and their most personal insider tips

„Ich trage immer extra so enggeschnürte Dirndl, damit ich von den vielen leckeren Sachen auf der Wiesn nicht so viel essen kann, so nehme ich nicht zu. Als Münchner Kindl liebe ich es mittags auf die Wiesn zu gehen, so wie es die alten Münchner früher gemacht haben. Um die Wiesn gut zu überstehen, trinke ich nur Apfelsaftschorle – die sieht aus wie Bier und man kann mit einem Krug anstoßen"

Regine Sixt

"I always wear a tight 'dirndl', because, with all these delicacies on offer at the Oktoberfest, I then can't eat that much. That way I don't put on weight. As a native from Munich I love to go to the 'Wiesn' at lunchtime, just as the old Munich locals once used to. In order to survive the festival I only drink 'Apfelsaftschorle' (apple juice and mineral water). It looks like beer and you can raise your mug with the others."

„Ich mag die Wiesn, weil man da bei einer Maß so schön entschleunigen kann. Aber ich fahr auch gern Achterbahn und hab' sogar einen Tipp, wie Ihnen nicht mulmig wird: Seien Sie locker, nicht verkrampfen. Wie im Leben – immer einfach mutig nach vorne schauen."

"I like the Oktoberfest because with beer in front of you it's so easy to slow down. But I also like to take a ride on the roller coaster and I have a tip on how to avoid being frightened: Stay calm, don't get tense. Like in everyday life—just look ahead with confidence."

Ralf Schumacher

Prinz Poldi von Bayern

„Mein Tipp ist ein Besuch beim Vogelbauer, der kleinsten Wiesn-Attraktion, gleich unter der Bavaria. Der Junge hat einfach die lustigsten Witze drauf. Außerdem verkauft er so Pfeiferln. Die legt man sich unter die Zunge, und dann kann man seiner Freundin oder seinem Freund hinterher pfeifen."

My tipp is to go and see Vogelbauer, the smallest stall at the 'Wiesn', just beneath the Bavaria statue. He always tells the funniest jokes and also sells small pipes which imitate birdsong. You put one of them underneath your tongue and then you can 'sing' to your girlfriend or boyfriend."

„Faszinierend auf der Wiesn finde ich ja diese Bierkrüge. Dass da so viel reingeht in einen! Als zarter Friese packt man den am besten mit beiden Händen an und versucht ihn dann hochzuhalten. Und langsam trinken, Leute. Denn dann steht gleich wieder ein frischer, neuer Krug da. Wichtig ist auch, dass man ganz, ganz eng zusammen sitzt, so dass man ganz, ganz viele nette Leute kennenlernt. Es geht schließlich um den Dialog. Und Platz haben wir zuhause."

Otto Waalkes

"What I find really fascinating at the Oktoberfest are these beer mugs. They hold so much liquid! Speaking as a delicate Frieslander from the North, I think it's best to grab the mug with both hands and try to raise it. And drink slowly, my friends, because suddenly a fresh, new mug will be put in front of you. It is also important to sit very, very close to each other, so that you get to know very, very many nice people. After all, it's all about conversation. Plenty of room to sit down ... we've got that at home."

„Die Wiesn ist nicht nur Gaudi, sondern hinter so manchem Bierkrug wird auch Business gemacht. Meine Empfehlung ist so: Nach der ersten Maß wird noch gepokert, nach der zweiten Maß kommt der wahre Charakter raus. Ab der dritten Maß sollte man nicht mehr geschäftlich reden, sondern sich nur noch dem Spaß widmen."

"The Oktoberfest is not just a lot of fun, but behind some of these beer mugs business is being done. My suggestion is: After the first mug of beer the contenders are still sparring. After the second their real characters show. After the third mug one really shouldn't talk business any more, but just enjoy oneself."

Boris Becker

„Ich bin schon deshalb ein großer Wiesn-Fan, weil ich dann meine schönen Dirndl anziehen kann. Für mich sind Dirndl einfach die bequemste „Verpackung" und doch unbeschreiblich weiblich. Mein Tipp: Lassen Sie sich eins bei „MB Style" in München-Schwabing machen. Melanie Baumgartner schneidert Unikate auf Maß, und die schönsten Mieder."

Veronica Ferres

"I'm such a big Oktoberfest fan because then I can put on my beautiful 'dirndls'. For me, 'dirndls' are simply the most comfortable 'wrapping' and so indescribably feminine. My tip: Get one made to measure at 'MB Style' in Schwabing (north Munich). Melanie Baumgartner makes unique garments to order, and the finest bodices as well."

„Wenn ich auf die Wiesn gehe, dann gehe ich nur mit meinen besten Freunden und auch mittenrein, also direkt vor die Kapelle. Denn dort, wo die Stimmung bebt, die Tische wackeln und man der Band quasi auf Augenhöhe zuprosten – und zuzwinkern – kann, erlebt man die Wiesn am besten. Da bin ich darum auch am liebsten und am glücklichsten, und singe mit – egal wie falsch."

"When I go to the Oktoberfest I go there only with my best friends, but I go right into the thick of it, directly in front of the band. Here, the atmosphere is really great, the tables dance and you raise your glasses to the band virtually at eye-level—and wink at them. This is the best way to experience the Oktoberfest. That's also why I'm so glad to be here, and so happy, and I sing along,—no matter how off-key."

Alexandra Flick

„Das Gesündeste ist es eigentlich, gar nicht auf die Wiesn zu gehen. Da ich mich aber selbst nicht an diesen Ratschlag halte, praktiziere ich bei meinem Besuch auf dem Oktoberfest immer die eiserne Faustregel: 1 Maß Bier, 1 Maß Wasser."

"The healthiest thing to do is not to go to the Oktoberfest at all. However, since I can't stick to this advice myself, I always strictly follow this strict regime when I go to the 'Wiesn': Alternating one mug of beer, one mug of water."

Franz Beckenbauer

„Wenn in München Oktoberfestzeit ist und alle Menschen lachen, tanzen und feiern, fühle ich mich meiner Heimat Brasilien so richtig nahe. Die Wiesn verbreitet gute Laune, so wie der Karneval in Rio. Mein Tipp: Mittags zu zweit über die Wiesn schlendern und gemütlich bei Sonnenschein Mittag essen. Gleichzeitig das prickelnde, aufregende Gefühl der vielen internationalen Gäste spüren, die in den nächsten Stunden die Wiesn-Zelte füllen werden, um alle gemeinsam – egal welche Kultur – Spaß zu haben."

"When in Munich the Oktoberfest period is in full swing and every one is laughing, dancing and partying, then I feel really close to my homeland, Brazil. The Oktoberfest spreads a good mood, just as the carnival in Rio does. My tip: Stroll around the Oktoberfest at midday with your partner, have lunch and relax together in the sunshine. At the same time you can enjoy the tingling, exciting feeling you get from all the international guests who will crowd the beer tents within the next few hours in order to have fun together—no matter where they are from."

Sônia Bogner

Wo gibt es die schönsten Trachten?

Chiemgauer oder Salzburger?
Maßgeschneidert oder von der Stange?
Oder vielleicht gar kein Dirndl?

11 Adressen für jeden Typ und Geldbeutel:

Where can you buy the best traditional clothes?

Chiemgau style or Salzburger?
Made to measure or off the peg?
Perhaps something other than a 'dirndl'?

Eleven addresses for every taste and every purse:

1 Loden-Frey

Ist das berühmteste Trachtenhaus Münchens mit der größten Auswahl an edelsten Marken wie Lanz („Sissy-Dirndl"), Stajan (die schönsten Loden-Jacken), Gössl (Blusen), Poldi- oder Habsburg-Tracht (fürstliche Trachtenmode), Meindl (Lederhosen). Preis: Dirndl nackt ab 195,- Euro, Lederhose ab 350,- Euro.

**Maffeistraße 7,
80333 München,
T: 089-21 03 90,
www.loden-frey.de**

1 Loden-Frey

Is Munich's most famous traditional clothes shop with the largest selection of the finest brand names such as Lanz ('Sissy-Dirndl'), Stajan (the finest 'loden' jackets), Gössl (blouses), Poldi- or Habsburg-Tracht (regal traditional fashions), Meindl ('lederhosen'). Prices: A dirndl on its own from €195 and 'lederhosen' from €350.

**Maffeistraße 7,
80333 Munich,
T: (++49)(0)89-21 03 90,
www.loden-frey.de**

2 Indra-Trachtenmoden

Ist die kleinste Maßschneiderei für schönste Dirndl. Auf 50 m² bieten Mutter Martha und Tochter Bobby über hundert Schnitte aus tausend Stoffen an. Dirndl ab 400,- Euro.

**Sparkassenstraße 10,
80331 München,
T: 089-22 01 63,
www.indra-trachtenmoden.de**

2 Indra-Trachtenmoden

Are the smallest tailors for the most beautiful made-to-order 'dirndls'. In 50 m² mother Martha and daughter Bobby have over a hundred patterns for a thousand different fabrics on offer.
A 'dirndl' from €400.

**Sparkassenstraße 10,
80331 Munich,
T: (++49)(0)89-22 01 63,
www.indra-trachtenmoden.de**

3 Lollipop & Alpenrock

Verkauft das alte Dirndl im neuen Gewand: schrill aufgestylte Designer-Trachten von Lola Paltinger, sowie Glitzer-T-Shirts mit bayerischen Applikationen. Dirndl ab 1800,- Euro.

**Tal 27, 80331 München,
T: 089-20 11 114,
www.lolapaltinger.com**

3 Lollipop & Alpenrock

Sells old-style 'dirndls' revamped: extravagantly exaggerated designer traditional clothes by Lola Paltinger and glitter T-shirts with Bavarian images in appliqué. A 'dirndl' from €1800.

**Tal 27, 80331 Munich,
T: (++49)(0)89-20 11 114,
www.lolapaltinger.com**

❹ Exatmo

Hat die extravaganten Trachten-Kombinationen: den „Captain-Cook“-Piraten-Look mit viel Leder, Rüschen und viel Bein. Mini statt maxi lautet hier das Dirndl-Motto. Preis: ab 1200,- Euro.

Franz-Joseph-Straße 35, 80801 München, T: 089-33 57 61, www.exatmo.de

❹ Exatmo

Has the most extravagant dress combinations: for instance a pirate look with loads of leather, frills and showing a lot of leg. Mini, not maxi is the motto for 'dirndls' in this shop. Prices from €1200.

Franz-Joseph-Straße 35, 80801 Munich, T: (++49)(0)89-33 57 61, www.exatmo.de

❺ Tracht und Heimat

Ist der wahre Trachten-Couturier mit der größten Auswahl an handbedruckten Seidentüchern. Hier werden auch Gehröcke, alle traditionellen Trachten und sogar Theaterkostüme angefertigt.

Oberanger 9, 80331 München, T: 089-26 04 321

❺ Tracht und Heimat

Is the ultimate costume couturier with the largest selection of hand printed silk scarves. All traditional clothes including frock coats and even theatre costumes are made here.

Oberanger 9, 80331 Munich, T: (++49)(0)89-26 04 321

❻ Angermaier Trachten

Schnell und preiswert findet sich hier das Komplett-Outfit, z.B. Landhaustrachten aus Leinen. Das Dirndl von der Stange (Bluse, Schürze inkl.) gibt's ab 119,- Euro.

Landsberger Str. 101–103, 80339 München, T: 089-50 16 77, www.trachten-angermaier.de

❻ Angermaier Trachten

A complete outfit is quickly found here, and for a reasonable price, e.g. linen country-style clothes. 'Dirndls' off the peg (blouse and apron included) from €119.

Landsberger Str.101–103, 80339 Munich, T. (++49)(0)89-50 16 77, www.trachten-angermaier.de

❼ Halfs

Hier gibt es den Halbschuh, also den Berg- oder Haferlschuh zur Tracht. 30 Modelle, handgenäht aus den Dolomiten in Leder, mit Fell oder Muster. Preis: ab 175,- Euro.

Prälat-Zistl-Straße. 7, 80331 München, T: 089-51 81 84 29, www.halfs.de

❼ Halfs

The Alpine loafer to accompany traditional costumes, known in German as 'Bergschuh' or 'Haferlschuh', can be found here. 30 different models, hand sewn, made of leather, with fur or patterns, produced in the Dolomites. Prices from €175.

Prälat-Zistl-Straße 7, 80331 Munich, T: (++49)(0)89-51 81 84 29, www.halfs.de

❽ Kult
Hier badet man in Modeschmuck, und findet witzige Accessoires zum Dirndl. Preis: ab 25,- Euro.
Hohenzollernstraße 40, 80801 München, T: 089-38 86 95 15

❽ Kult
You could almost drown in costume jewellery here and find funny accessories for your 'dirndl'. Prices from €25.
Hohenzollernstraße 40, 80801 Munich, T: (++49)(0)89-38 86 95 15

❾ Servus Heimat
Begrüßt alle Jeans-Fans ohne Lust auf große Tracht mit frech bedruckten Wiesn-T-Shirts. Preis: ab 25,- Euro.
Ledererstraße 17, 80331 München, T: 089-24 29 47 80, www.servusheimat.com

❾ Servus Heimat
For all fans of jeans who are not too much into traditional clothes. Also Wiesn-T-shirts with daring prints. Prices from €25.
Ledererstraße 17, 80331 Munich, T: (++49)(0)89-24 29 47 80, www.servusheimat.com

❿ Luis Trenker & Friends
Bietet trachtige Retro-Mode für Jung und Alt. Schnitte aus den 30ern und 60ern: Knickerbocker, Karohemden. Das Alternativ-Outfit für die Wiesn. Preis: ab 300,- Euro.
Hohenzollernstraße 62, 80801 München, T: 089-38 88 90 12, www.luistrenker-muenchen.de

❿ Luis Trenker & Friends
Offers traditional-style retro clothes for all generations. Patterns from the 1930s and 1960s: plus-fours, checked shirts. Alternative outfits for the Oktoberfest. Prices from €300.
Hohenzollernstraße 62, 80801 Munich, T: (++49)(0)89-38 88 90 12, www.luistrenker-muenchen.de

⓫ Holareidulijö
Sammelt vor allem Antikes und Getragenes vom Schuh bis zum Hut, wie alte Lederhosen und Leinenhemden. Darunter Raritäten wie Dachauer Stiefelhosen von 1880. Preis ab: 50,- Euro.
Schellingstraße 81, 80799 München, T: 089-2 71 77 45, www.holareidulijoe.com

⓫ Holareidulijö
Collects mainly antique and second hand items, from shoes to hats, such as old 'lederhosen' and linen shirts. Also rarities such as Dachauer Stiefelhosen (boot pants) dating from 1880. Prices from €50.
Schellingstrasse 81, 80799 Munich, T: (++49)(0)89-2 71 77 45, www.holareidulijoe.com

Die Zelte

Tents

Wiesn-Plan

1 Hippodrom
2 Armbrustschützen-Festhalle
3 Hofbräu-Festzelt
4 Hackerbräu-Festhalle
5 Schottenhamel-Festz
6 Winzerer Fähndl
7 Schützen-Festhalle
8 Käfer's Wies'n Schän
9 Weinzelt

Map

0 Löwenbräu-Festhalle
1 Bräurosl
2 Augustiner-Festhalle
3 Ochsenbraterei
4 Fischer-Vroni
15 Bodo's Backstube
16 Hühner- und Entenbraterei AMMER
17 Bratwurst Glöckl
18 Münchner Knödelei

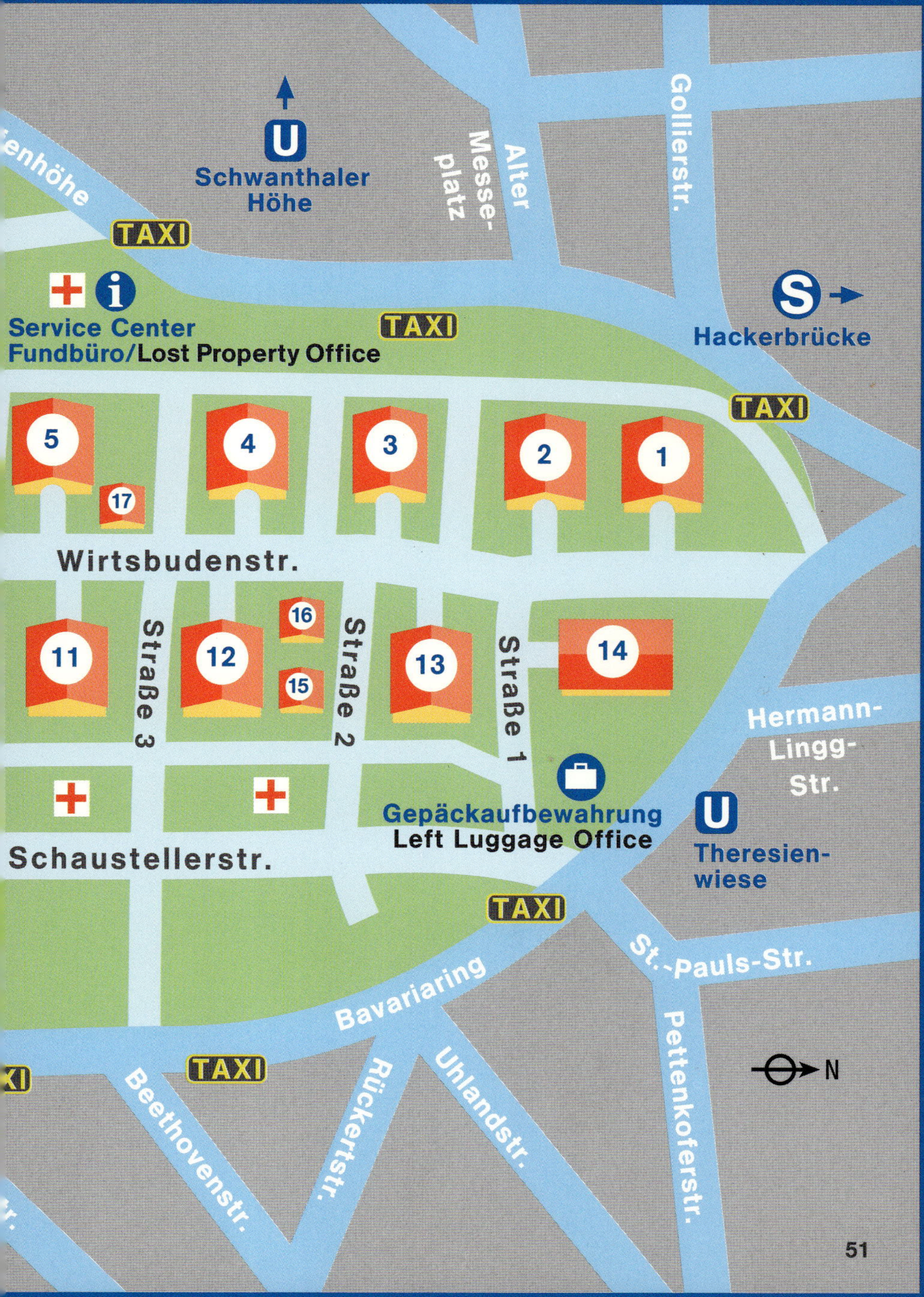

Hippodrom

Im Hippodrom wird gekuckt, ob jemand kuckt

⧫ **Historie** ⧫ Hippodrom ist griechisch und steht für: Reitbahn. Früher durften hier nämlich die Damen für 50 Pfennig auf geduldigen Vierbeinern ihre Runden drehen, während die Herren damals noch elegant am Sekt, aber manche auch schon am ersten Bier nippten und winkten.

⧫ **Atmosphäre** ⧫ So in etwa sieht eine Bayerische Filmkulisse aus: Schäumendes Bier auf bunt gedeckten Tischen. Kellnerinnen, die in Spitzen-Dirndln knusprig duftende Schweinsbraten auf ihren zarten Schultern tragen. Und an der Champagner-Bar giggelt ab 16 Uhr Münchens Schickeria oder die, die sich dafür halten beim Kultdrink „Be in love" aus pürierten Himbeeren. Da wird kräftig angebandelt!

⧫ **Zelt-Philosophie** ⧫ Das Hippodrom ist eines der schillernden Prominentenzelte, wie ein roter Teppich. Ein Laufsteg zum Bier. Jeder Besuch ist ein Event. Hier finden auch Gourmets ihren Platz – vor frischen Waldpilzen oder Hendl in Andechser Fassbutter. Aber hinter so manchem Bussi-Bussi oder Bier wird auch schweres Business gemacht.

⧫ **Wer hier sitzt** ⧫ Schauspieler und Agenten, Künstler und Produzenten. Veronica Ferres (liebt Fleischpflanzerl in der Schichtl-Box), Produzent Bernd Eichinger (thront in der Burda-Verleger-Box auf der Galerie mit dem besten Blick); Bayerns TV- und Filmgesellschaft – weil im Hippodrom auch die Presse hockt. Also auch Boris Becker mit Freundin – wenn er gesehen werden will.

In the Hippodrom you see and are seen

⧫ **History** ⧫ The word 'hippodrom' is Greek and means riding arena. In the early years the ladies were able to ride patient horses for 50 pfennig. While the gentlemen would in those days elegantly sip at their sparkling wine, although some already had their first beer and would wave at the ladies.

⧫ **Atmosphere** ⧫ A Bavarian film set would look something like this: Frothing beer on colourful tablecloths. Waitresses in fine lace 'dirndls' carrying trays of crispy, aromatic 'schweinsbraten' on their delicate shoulders. From 4 pm, at the champagne bar, Munich's glitterati, or at least those who think they are, are giggling and sipping the cult drink 'Be in Love' made from pureed raspberries. A lot of chatting up is going on!

⧫ **Tent philosophy** ⧫ The Hippodrom is one of the most colourful celebrity beer tents. It is a red carpet in itself, like a catwalk on the way to the bar. Every visit is an event. Gourmets are also at the right address–they are served fresh, wild mushrooms or chicken roasted in hand-made butter from Andechs. But behind the beer some serious business is being conducted.

⧫ **Who comes here** ⧫ Actors and agents, artists and producers, the actress Veronica Ferres is served in the Schichtl-box, and producer Bernd Eichinger, resides in the house box of a big publishing house (Burda) up on the gallery. Bavaria's TV and film community is here–because the press frequents the Hippodrom. Therefore Boris Becker with girlfriend makes

♦ **Besonderheit** ♦ Im Hippodrom wird nicht nur sündig gefeiert, sondern auch gebetet: Immer am ersten Wiesndonnerstag um 10 Uhr findet hier ein Gottesdienst statt, allerdings nur für die Wiesnwirte und Schausteller, die in einem ökumenischen Gottesdienst auch ihre Kinder taufen lassen können. Lauschen Sie ruhig mal an der Zeltwand: dann können sie Pfarrer Heller hören, einen Schweizer, der fantastisch jodelt und Klarinette spielt.

♦ **Der Wirt** ♦ Sepp Krätz ist Wirt mit Leib und Seele. Man kriegt den Mann zwar von der Wiesn, aber die Wiesn nie aus diesem Mann. Hinter den Kulissen führt er ein strenges Regiment, aber auf seiner Bier-Bühne beherrscht er das Bussi-Bussi wie kein anderer.

♦ **Events** ♦ Hier trifft sich jedes Jahr der BILD-Stammtisch, die größte Boulevard-Zeitung mit Deutschlands Show-Prominenz, und Boris Becker begießt seine karitative „Golf-Trophy".

an appearance–if he wants to be seen.

♦ **Special feature** ♦ The Hippodrom is not only a place for celebration; it is also a place for worship: Each year, on the first Thursday at ten, a church service takes place but it is only for the tent managers and the personnel of the fairground attractions, who may also have their children christened during an ecumenical service. You can easily eavesdrop at the side of the tent and you will hear Pastor Heller who is a fantastic yodeller and clarinet player.

♦ **The manager** ♦ Sepp Krätz is a beer tent manager with his heart and soul. He has the 'Wiesn' in his blood. Behind the scenes he rules with a strict hand but in the tent he knows how to work the crowd like no other.

♦ **Events** ♦ Each year the editors of Germany's biggest tabloid daily, the BILD newspaper, meet show-biz celebrities at their regular table, and Boris Becker drinks to his charitable 'golf trophy'.

Hippodrom

Festwirte: Gabi und Sepp Krätz
Reservierungsbüro:
T: 089-29 16 46 46, F: 089-29 54 42
Zeltbüro:
T: 089-500 77 550, F: 089-500 77 553
Sitzplätze: 4200
Brauerei: Spaten-Franziskaner-Bräu
Musik: Münchner Zwietracht, Simmisamma.
www.hippodrom-oktoberfest.de

Tent managers: Gabi and Sepp Krätz
Reservations: (country code ++49)
T: (0) 89-29 16 46 46, F: (0) 89-29 54 42
Tent office: (country code ++49)
T: (0) 89-500 77 550, F: (0) 89-500 77 553
Seating capacity: 4,200
Brewery: Spaten-Franziskaner-Bräu
Music: Münchner Zwietracht, Simmisamma
www.hippodrom-oktoberfest.de

Hippodrom

Armbrustschützen-Festhalle

In der Armbrustschützen-Festhalle treffen sich die mutigen Schürzenjäger

♦ **Historie** ♦ Die Armbrustschützen-Festhalle hat ihren Namen, weil sie seit 110 Jahren eine eigene Schützenanlage hat. Hier schießen heute noch die Schützen in mittelalterlicher Tracht.

♦ **Atmosphäre** ♦ Könnte man die Armbrustschützen-Festhalle rahmen, sie wäre das Gemälde einer fröhlichen, Loden tragenden Jagdgesellschaft: junge Schützen und alte Jagdherren beim Haxenbraten-Mahl. Das hat Tradition und viel Stil. Alle Boxen tragen übrigens Wildnamen. Nur für den Buchstaben „N" gibt's noch keinen („Nashorn" zählt nicht). Wem einer einfällt, der kriegt Freibier, hat die Wirtin versprochen.

♦ **Zelt-Philosophie** ♦ Wer auf diesen Bänken sitzt, der sucht keinen Star. Der will das echte, ur-gesellige Münchnerische: Eine gemütliche Dorfkrug-Atmosphäre und bayerische Gastfreundschaft – ohne Extrawürste und Tamtam.

♦ **Wer hier sitzt** ♦ Hier schunkelt der konservative Gaudianer, das alte München und die gute, gediegene Vorortgesellschaft. Der Oberförster und die Landratstochter, sowie einmal im Jahr Münchens Bäckermeister. Und die Italiener kommen gern hierher. Angeblich wegen der Dirndl-Farben der Bedienungen in rot-weiß-grün ...

In the Armbrustschützen-Festhalle the gallant philanderers convene

♦ **History** ♦ This 'crossbow men's festive hall' is called like that because it has had its own crossbow shooting gallery for over 110 years. Even today crossbow men still compete dressed in medieval costume.

♦ **Atmosphere** ♦ If it were possible to put the scene in the Armbrustschützen beer tent into a frame, it would make a fine traditional picture of cheerful huntsmen in their 'loden' coats: young crossbow men and elderly huntsmen eating their roast dinner together, very traditional and sophisticated. All the boxes are called after wild game. Only for the letter 'N' there is no name yet. If you can think of one (in German of course) the manageress has promised free beer.

♦ **Tent philosophy** ♦ Whoever comes here is not looking for celebrities. They are after the real, original Munich community: A pleasant, village-green atmosphere and Bavarian hospitality–without any special treats or fuss.

♦ **Who comes here** ♦ Sitting here are the rather more conservative guests enjoying themselves, the old Munich and the good, descent people from the suburbs: The head forester, the councillor's daughter and also once a year Munich's master bakers. The Italians gladly come here as well, apparently due

Peppi & Peter F. J. Inselkammer

♦ **Besonderheit** ♦ Firmen bis zu 150 Personen können in der Armbrustschützen-Festhalle buchen, um sich im Armbrustschießen zu messen. Der Verlierer muss übrigens auf einen Radi, einen Rettich, zielen. Geht das auch daneben, wird er mit 50 Liter Paulaner-Freibier bitter bestraft.

♦ **Die Wirte** ♦ Peter Inselkammer, ein Bayer im feinen Loden, und Peppi, seine witzige Ehefrau. Sie lauert meist in der „Pirsch"-Box, weshalb diese auch die beliebteste ist.

♦ **Events** ♦ Hier findet jedes Jahr die deutsche Meisterschaft im Armbrustschützenschießen statt.

to the waitresses 'dirndl' colours of red, white and green ...

♦ **Special feature** ♦ Companies or groups of up to 150 people can book the Festhalle, and put their marksmanship to the test with crossbows. The loser, incidentally, must then shoot at a 'radi', a white radish, and if he misses again he forfeits 50 litres of free Paulaner beer.

♦ **The managers** ♦ Peter Inselkammer, a Bavarian in fine 'loden', and Peppi, his witty wife. She is usually to be found in the 'Pirsch' box, which makes this box the favourite with everybody.

♦ **Events** ♦ Every year the German crossbow championships take place here.

Armbrustschützen-Festhalle

Festwirte:
Peter, Peppi und Peter F. J. Inselkammer
Reservierungsbüro:
T: 089-23 70 37 03, F: 089-23 70 37 05
Zeltbüro:
T: 089-500 77 300, F: 089-500 77 302
Sitzplätze: 7430
Brauerei: Paulaner
Musik: Unterbrunner Blasmusik, Die Unterbrunner Haderlumpen
www.armbrustschuetzenzelt.de

Tent managers:
Peter, Peppi and Peter F. J. Inselkammer
Reservations: (country code ++49)
T: (0) 89-23 70 37 03, F: (0) 89-23 70 37 05
Tent office: (country code ++49)
T: (0) 89-500 77 300, F: (0) 89-500 77 302
Seating capacity: 7,430
Brewery: Paulaner
Music: Unterbrunner Blasmusik, Die Unterbrunner Haderlumpen
www.armbrustschuetzenzelt.de

Schottenhamel-Festzelt

Im Schottenhamel küsst die Jugend nicht nur ihr erstes Bier

♦ Historie ♦ Es ist das älteste Zelt der Wiesn. Der alte Schottenhamel war befreundet mit dem damaligen Bürgermeister Thomas Wimmer. Der Wirt erfand damals die Geste, dass der Oberbürgermeister in seinem Zelt das erste Bierfass anschlägt. Wimmer brauchte 1950 noch 30 Schläge. OB Ude hält heute den Rekord mit dreien.

♦ Atmosphäre ♦ Obwohl das Zelt schon seine 175 Jahre auf dem Buckel hat, ist es der Treffpunkt der Jugend: Trinken ist hier die eine Sache. Reden und Kontakten die andere. Und das geht so: Rund um die Blaskapelle tummeln sich die Abitur-Frischlinge internationaler Elite-Internate und halten Ausschau nach adrettem Flirt-Material.

♦ Zelt-Philosophie ♦ Der Schottenhamel ist mit seinem dunklen Holz und weiß-blauen Bänderschmuck eine Hommage an Bayern. Wie ein überdachtes Waldfest, bei dem man seine vier Buchstaben ganz locker neben beste Partien, ja, sogar ganze Konzerne platzieren kann.

♦ Wer hier sitzt ♦ Studentenverbindungen. Die „goldenen Löffel“, die nicht selten noch grün hinter den selbigen sind. Dazu oben, auf der Empore, die Herren vom Stadtrat. Und unten alte Familien wie die Schottenhamels selbst.

In the Schottenhamel beer tent the young kiss not only their first beer

♦ History ♦ It is the oldest tent of the 'Wiesn'. Old Herr Schottenhamel was a friend of the then mayor Thomas Wimmer. He invented the tradition that the mayor has to tap the first barrel in **his** tent. Back then in 1950 Thomas Wimmer took 30 mallet strikes to fix the barrel's tap. At the moment mayor Christian Ude holds the record, needing only three.

♦ Atmosphere ♦ Although this tent is about 175 years old it is the favourite of the young. Drinking in here is one thing, talking and networking is the other. This is how it goes: All around the brass band the high school graduates of international elite boarding schools flock around and keep a look out for pretty flirting material.

♦ Tent philosophy ♦ The Schottenhamel beer tent, with its dark wooden panelling and blue-and-white garland ribbons, is homage to Bavaria. Something like a sheltered party in the woods where you can park your posterior quite easily next to the rich and famous, the best of company, yes, even next to whole corporations.

♦ Who comes here ♦ Students' societies; those born with a silver spoon in their mouths who are incidentally still wet behind their ears. Also, upstairs on the gallery, the gentlemen of the city council, and down below, old families as the Schottenhamels themselves.

Peter & Christian Schottenhamel

♦ Besonderheit ♦ In diesem Zelt hat einst Albert Einstein als Lehrling einer Münchner Elektrofirma die Glühbirnen eingedreht. Man sagt heute noch, wer einmal in den Schottenhamel geht, dem geht ein Lichtlein auf ...
♦ Die Wirte ♦ Peter und Christian Schottenhamel sind die „Wellnis" auf der Wiesn: sie lassen sich gern mal Sushi kommen und Vitamine gegen Erschöpfung spritzen.
♦ Events ♦ Der Anstich am ersten Wiesnsamstag. Punkt zwölf ruft hier der Oberbürgermeister: O'zapft is!

♦ Special feature ♦ In this tent, employed by a Munich electrical company and screwing in the light bulbs, Albert Einstein once worked as an apprentice. Still today you can hear people say that if you go to the Schottenhamel tent you will see the light ...
♦ The managers ♦ Peter and Christian Schottenhamel are the wellness team at the Oktoberfest: They are quite happy to have sushi delivered and inject vitamins to keep exhaustion at bay.
♦ Events ♦ The opening ceremony with the traditional tapping of the first beer barrel on the first day. At the stroke of twelve the mayor shouts: "O'zapft is!" (The barrel is tapped).

Schottenhamel-Festzelt

Festwirte:
Peter und Christian Schottenhamel
Reservierungsbüro:
T: 089-54 46 93 10, F: 089-54 46 93 19
Zeltbüro:
T: 089-500 77 372, F: 089-500 77 382
Sitzplätze innen: 10 000
Brauerei: Spaten-Franziskaner-Bräu
Musik: Kapelle Otto Schwarzfischer
www.festzelt.schottenhamel.de

Tent managers:
Peter and Christian Schottenhamel
Reservations: (country code ++49)
T: (0) 89-54 46 93 10, F: (0) 89-54 46 93 19
Tent office: (country code ++49)
T: (0) 89-500 77 372, F: (0) 89-500 77 382
Seating capacity: 10,000
Brewery: Spaten-Franziskaner-Bräu
Music: Kapelle Otto Schwarzfischer
www.festzelt.schottenhammel.de

Hofbräu-Festzelt

Im Hofbräu-Festzelt feie-l-n die Japane-l und Stoiber seinen Geburtstag

♦ **Historie** ♦ Das Hofbräuhaus in Münchens Innenstadt ist die ehemalige Brauereisudstätte der bayerischen Herzöge und Könige. Ihr Bier fließt heute noch im Hofbräu-Festzelt auf der Wiesn, wo viele Europareisen für Touristen mit einer Maß enden.

♦ **Atmosphäre** ♦ Zünftig, laut, rustikal. Hier macht man keine langen Sätze. Darum aufgepasst beim Bier! Das Personal ist flink: Halbvolle Krüge gelten als leer und werden zackig ausgetauscht gegen frische. Ganz so wie es dem alten Franz Josef Strauß gefiel. Deshalb war das Hofbräu-Festzelt auch sein Lieblingszelt.

♦ **Zelt-Philosophie** ♦ Ist ein Kommando und geht so: Zicke-zacke-zicke-zacke-hoi-hoi-hoi. Sofort stemmen alle ihre Krüge. Dann macht es kling-klang-klong – und alles trinkt. Um nichts anderes geht es hier. Das Hofbräu-Festzelt ist eine „Großraum-Tränke". Hier steht man darum gern auch mal, besonders vor der Blaskapelle, bis man so stramme Wadln hat wie die Bedienungen.

♦ **Wer hier sitzt** ♦ Die durstige Invasion aus Japan, Australien und USA. Mehr oder weniger trinkfeste Touristen mit leichtem Hang zum Exhibitionismus aus aller Welt. Aber auch die Bayern trauen sich noch hierher. Der Mix macht genau die Stimmung.

The Hofbräu beer tent is known for its Japanese visitors and the Bavarian premier's birthday party

♦ **History** ♦ The Hofbräuhaus in Munich's city centre is on the site of the former brewhouse of the Bavarian dukes' and kings' brewery. Its beer is served to this day in the Hofbräu beer tent at the Oktoberfest, where many tourists end their tour of Europe with a pint of beer.

♦ **Atmosphere** ♦ Excellent, loud, rustic. Here you will find the conversation very fast. Not only the conversation: Watch out for your beer! The personnel are quick: half-full beer mugs are considered empty and are rapidly exchanged for full ones. This is just how a former Bavarian premier, the late Franz Josef Strauss, liked it. That is why the Hofbräu tent was his favourite.

♦ **Tent philosophy** ♦ It is a command and this is how it goes: "Zicke-zacke-zicke-zacke-hoi-hoi-hoi." Now everyone lifts their mugs. Then you hear a loud 'cling-clang-clong' and everybody takes a swig. That is what it is all about. The Hofbräu tent is one big watering hole. Here you can stand right in front of the brass band for a while, until your legs become as fit as the waitresses' legs.

♦ **Who comes here** ♦ The thirsty visitors from Japan, Australia and the US; people from all over the world who can more or less hold their drink and who show a slight tendency towards exhibitionism. Even Bavarians are still bold enough to

Margot & Günter Steinberg

♦ **Besonderheit** ♦ Bayerns Ministerpräsident Edmund Stoiber feiert im Hofbräu-Festzelt gern seinen Geburtstag um den 28. September mit frischem Hendl, Kaiserschmarrn und der ganzen Familie: in der Wirte-Box rechts außen, wo ihm jeder gratulieren kann.

♦ **Die Wirte** ♦ Wiesenwirtin Margot Steinberg hat so viel Herz wie ein Bergwerk. Sie ist die gute Seele des Familienbetriebes. Rührend wird's am letzten Abend, wenn die ganze Familie Steinberg auf die Bühne geht und mit allen Gästen das letzte Lied singt. Da bleibt kein Auge trocken.

♦ **Events** ♦ Margot Steinbergs privates Wiesn-Kaffeekränzchen mit Bienenstich und Obsttorte und allen 14 Festzeltwirtinnen in der Hausbox.

come here. It is exactly this mixture that creates the mood.

♦ **Special feature** ♦ Bavaria's premier Edmund Stoiber always celebrates his birthday here in the Hofbräu tent on 28 September with his family. He has fresh chicken, 'Kaiserschmarrn' and sits in the manager's box on the far right-hand side where anyone can come up to him to congratulate.

♦ **The managers** ♦ Margot Steinberg, the manageress, has a heart as big as a house. She is the heart and soul of this family business. The last evening is usually very touching when all members of the Steinberg family get up onto the stage to sing the last song along with all the guests. Not a single eye remains dry.

♦ **Events** ♦ Margot Steinberg has her own private party with coffee and 'Bienenstich' in the house box and invites all 14 beer tent manageresses.

Hofbräu-Festzelt

Festwirte: Margot und Günter Steinberg
Reservierungsbüro:
T: 089-448 96 70, F: 089-448 35 87
Zeltbüro:
T: 089-50 07 75 66, F: 089-50 22 22 36
Sitzplätze: 10 000
Brauerei: Hofbräu
Musik: Plattlinger Isarspatzen
www.hb-festzelt.de

Tent managers: Margot and Günter Steinberg
Reservations: (country code ++49)
T: (0) 89-448 96 70, F: (0) 89-448 35 87
Tent office: (country code ++49)
T: (0) 89-50 07 75 66, F: (0) 89-50 22 22 36
Seating capacity: 10,000
Brewery: Hofbräu
Music: Plattlinger Isarspatzen
www.hb-festzelt.de

Hackerbräu-Festhalle

Alles ist herrlich blau in der Hackerbräu-Festhalle

♦ **Historie** ♦ Wenn Sie sehen wollen, was ein Oscar-Gewinner aus dem „Himmel der Bayern“ gemacht hat, besuchen Sie die Hackerbräu-Festhalle. Rolf Zehetbauer, der 1972 den Oscar für die Cabaret-Filmkulisse bekam, hat die berühmte Zeltdecke gestaltet.

♦ **Atmosphäre** ♦ Hier ist schon mittags alles herrlich blau: Über der goldenen Maß leuchtet die himmelblaue Zeltdecke, als ob die Englein Badetag haben. Und genau darum, weil der Himmel niemandem grau auf den Kopf fällt, und auch die Band so super aufspielt, hat jeder hier einfach gute Laune.

♦ **Zelt-Philosophie** ♦ In der Hackerbräu-Festhalle ist es noch wie es früher war, als man vor allem am hellen Tag auf die Wiesn kam: Das Hendl kommt als Nackedei, ohne einen Dialog von Gurke an Zitrone. Getrunken wird weder aus Stein, noch aus Plastik, sondern aus dem Glaskrug. Und die Kapelle hält sich an den Brauch: Bis 18 Uhr wird geblasen, erst dann rockt die Band.

♦ **Wer hier sitzt** ♦ Die Pfundigen und die Vorabend-Gesellschaft: Serien-Lieblinge wie Christine Neubauer und Ottfried Fischer. Und eigentlich schaut jeder Politiker auch mal vorbei, um ein Hacker Bier zu heben.

Everything is heavenly blue in the Hackerbräu-Festhalle

♦ **History** ♦ If you would like to see what an Oscar winner made of the ‘Himmel der Bayern’ (Bavarians’ heaven) then visit this beer tent, the Hackerbräu-Festhalle. Rolf Zehetbauer, who won an Oscar for the set design in the film ‘Cabaret’ in 1972, also designed the famous ceiling of this tent.

♦ **Atmosphere** ♦ Already at midday everything is heavenly blue here: High above the golden beer mug, the sky-blue ceiling shines, as if little cherubs were enjoying a day of bathing. The bright ceiling keeps the grey skies away and the band plays so well that everyone here is always in a good mood.

♦ **Tent philosophy** ♦ In the Hackerbräu-Festhalle everything is as it once used to be, when visitors mainly used to come during the day: ‘Hendl’ (grilled chicken) is served without any frills like cucumber or lemon. Drinks are served neither in earthenware ‘steins’ nor in plastic, but are served in glass mugs. The band as well adheres to tradition: they are a brass bank until six in the evening, only then do they turn into a rock band.

♦ **Who comes here** ♦ The swell and early-evening TV people: TV celebrities such as Christine Neubauer and Ottfried Fischer, and many a politician are known to drop in and raise a mug of Hacker beer.

Christl & Toni Roiderer

♦ **Besonderheit** ♦ Die Besonderheit in der Hackerbräu-Festhalle ist: Dass es keine Besonderheit gibt. Hier ist alles noch herrlich „normal". Das ist ja gerade die Rarität. Darum berichtet auch der Bayerische Rundfunk täglich live von hier, von der Empore.

♦ **Die Wirte** ♦ Wiesn-Wirt Toni Roiderer ist gleichzeitig Sprecher aller Wiesnwirte, ein echter Kommunikator und Oberbayer, für den Bierkrüge wie Kirchenglocken klingen. Ein Zeichen, dass alle nächstenlieb und zufrieden sind.

♦ **Event** ♦ Nicht nur im Schottenhamel-Festzelt wird Punkt 12 das Anzapfen am 1. Wiesn-Samstag groß gefeiert, sondern nun auch seit mehr als 12 Jahren in der Hackerbräu-Festhalle. Wenn nämlich Toni Roiderers bullenstarker Freund Ottfried Fischer mit viel Kraft und manchmal 10 Schlägen das erste Bierfass anzapft und „O'zapft is" hinausposaunt.

♦ **Special feature** ♦ The special feature is that there is none. Here everything is still delightfully 'normal' and that is already something quite rare. That is the reason why the Bayerische Rundfunk (Bavarian TV and radio network) reports from here every day, from the gallery.

♦ **The manager** ♦ Tent manager Toni Roiderer is from Upper Bavaria and also the speaker for all the beer tent managers, a gifted communicator and so the clang of the beer mugs sounds like music to him—a sign that all his guests are benevolent and content.

♦ **Events** ♦ On the first Saturday at noon the tapping of the first beer barrel has been celebrated not only in the Schottenhamel-Festzelt but also in the Hackerbräu-Festhalle, for more than 12 years now. Toni Roiderer's stout friend, Bavarian actor Ottfried Fischer, taps the first barrel with all his might. He sometimes needs as many as 10 strikes before he shouts "O'zapft is!".

Hackerbräu-Festhalle

Festwirte: Christl und Toni Roiderer
Reservierungsbüro:
T: 08170-73 03, F: 08170-73 85
Zeltbüro:
T: 089-50 22 22 40 , F: 089-50 22 22 30
Plätze: 9350
Brauerei: Hacker Pschorr
Musik: Cagey Strings Rock'n'Roll Band

Tent managers: Christl and Toni Roiderer
Reservations: (country code ++49)
T: (0) 8170-73 03, F: (0) 8170-73 85
Tent office: (country code ++49)
T: (0) 89-50 22 22 40, F: (0) 89-50 22 22 30
Seating capacity: 9,350
Brewery: Hacker Pschorr
Music: Cagey Strings Rock'n'Roll Band

Hackerbräu-Festhalle

Winzerer Fähndl

Das sonnige Winzerer Fähndl zieht die feschen Bienen an

♦ **Historie** ♦ Das Winzerer Fähndl ist das sogenannte Sonnenzelt, weil es seinen Garten auf der Südseite hat. Da grillt man knusprig-braun wie ein Hendl am Spieß.

♦ **Atmosphäre** ♦ Sonnig, wie auf einer Blüte, mit gelbem Dach und gelbem Bänderschmuck. Die Luft schmeckt zwar nicht nach Nektar, aber es duftet optisch so. Die Stimmen summen, die Stimmung swingt. Und noch eins ist dieses Zelt: eines der wenigen ohne Häusl-Stau. Weil man sich dort nämlich nicht zum Dauertelefonieren in die Zellen verpieseln kann – was gern in Zelten gemacht wird. Der Wirt hat extra das Funknetz gestört.

♦ **Zelt-Philosophie** ♦ Es ist das Zelt ohne Alter. Ob junge Biene oder alter Bock, der neue Wiesn-Wirt hat nur ein Motto: 'ne gute Gaudi, aber bitte ohne Gesichtsentgleisung.

♦ **Wer hier sitzt** ♦ Die Belegschaft des FC-Bayern feiert hier jedes Jahr auf der Galerie. Das Paulaner ist schließlich Bayern-Sponsor. Auch Sonnenanbeter Blacky Fuchsberger kommt gern (wegen des Teints), und Münchens Mode-Diva Rudolf Mooshammer begoss oft seinen Geburtstag hier.

♦ **Besonderheit** ♦ Nicht nur, dass Küchenchef Andreas Geitl den besten Kaiserschmarrn macht. Er flambiert ihn in einer guss-

The sunny Winzerer Fähndl attracts the hip sun lovers

♦ **History** ♦ The Winzerer Fähndl tent is also known as the sun tent because its beer garden is on the southern side of the tent. If the weather is good you can get a sun tan while you enjoy the beer.

♦ **Atmosphere** ♦ Sunny, like a summer meadow, with a yellow roof and yellow ribbons and garlands. The air may not quite taste like nectar but the optical impression creates the illusion at least. Conversations are humming and the atmosphere is buzzing. Yet, there is one more side to this tent: It is one of the few without a queue for the toilets. The reason: It is no longer possible to use a mobile phone in the cubicles, where people usually go to get some peace and quiet (by the way many happily still phone in the tents). The manager has blocked reception.

♦ **Tent philosophy** ♦ It is the tent without an age. Whether you are young and hip or old and grey, the new manager has just one motto: Have a lot of fun, but please do not binge drink.

♦ **Who comes here** ♦ Every year Bayern Munich celebrates here on the gallery. The Paulaner brewery is the football team's sponsor after all. Celebrity sun worshippers as Blacky Fuchsberger, are known to come here, and Munich's fashion guru, Rudolf Mooshammer, often used to celebrate his birthdays here.

Arabella & Peter Pongratz

eisernen Riesen-Pfanne direkt in der Box vor dem Gast – der Feuerlöscher steht immer in greifbarer Nähe!

♦ Die Wirte ♦ Peter und Arabella Pongratz sind selbst die fleißigsten Bienchen. Er leitet übrigens auch den „Nockherberg“, Bayerns Starkbierhochburg.
Von wegen: Wer nichts wird, wird Wirt.

♦ Events ♦ Es wirkt immer, als wäre der „Weiße Riese“ Gastgeber, wenn jedes Jahr 600 Dirndl ein anderes Wiesn-Zelt zur „Damen-Wiesn“ von Unternehmerin Regine Sixt überfluten. Einlass ist leider nur mit persönlicher Einladung. Und die Buam müssen draußen bleiben.

♦ Special feature ♦ Not only does chef Andreas Geitl make the best Kaiserschmarrn (chopped, sugared pancake with raisins), he flambés them in a large cast-iron frying pan in front of the guests in their private box. The fire extinguisher is always at hand!

♦ The managers ♦ Peter and Arabella Pongratz are themselves the busiest bees: Peter incidentally also runs the Nockherberg, the flagship of Bavaria's strong-beer festival.

♦ Events ♦ Each year it seems as if a washing powder advert was being shot: when, one day at lunchtime, 600 'dirndl' flood a tent, the Winzerer Fähndl for instance, at the 'Damen-Wiesn' (ladies Oktoberfest) hosted by business woman Regine Sixt. Admission is only by personal invitation. And the boys are not allowed in.

Winzerer Fähndl

Festwirte: Arabella und Peter Pongratz
Reservierungsbüro:
T: 089-62 17 19 10, F: 089-62 17 19 19
Zeltbüro:
T: 089-50 22 22 00, F: 089-50 22 22 02
Sitzplätze: 11 000
Brauerei: Paulaner
Musik: Nockherberger

Tent managers: Arabella and Peter Pongratz
Reservations: (country code ++49)
T: (0) 89-62 17 19 10, F: (0) 89-62 17 19 19
Tent office: (country code ++49)
T: (0) 89-50 22 22 00, F: (0) 89-50 22 22 02
Seating capacity: 11,000
Brewery: Paulaner
Music: Nockherberger

Schützen-Festhalle

In der Schützen-Festhalle heißt man wie ein Land oder eine Firma

♦ **Historie** ♦ Es ist das Zelt der Schützenvereine mit über 100 Schießständen. Hier schunkelt auch Deutschlands Adel.

♦ **Atmosphäre** ♦ Hier steht man gewissermaßen im zweiten Wohnzimmer der jungen Wilden und alten Aristokraten. Vor allem an den Wochenenden ist es hier mittags schon so voll, dass kein Dirndl mehr reinpasst.

♦ **Zelt-Philosophie** ♦ Ein Zelt wie ein Zuhause, wo man sich kennt und unter sich bleibt, also quasi heimkommt. Fast jeder ist auch irgendwie mit jedem verwandt. Und wenn nicht, dann heiratet man sich ein paar Wiesn später.

♦ **Wer hier sitzt** ♦ Familie v. Bayern gepaart mit welchen, die heißen wie ein Bleistift oder eine Babynahrung. Die Wirtin drückt es allgemeiner und so aus: „Alles, was sich 50 Kilometer um einen bayerischen Kirchturm bewegt", sagt sie. Dabei hat sie allerdings die Hamburger

In the Schützen-Festhalle the guests' surnames sound like countries or companies

♦ **History** ♦ The Schützen-Festhalle is the shooting clubs' beer tent with over 100 shooting galleries. Germany's nobility and aristocracy are also known to drink here.

♦ **Atmosphere** ♦ In some way you are here in the second drawing room of the Bright Young Things and old aristocrats. Mainly at the weekends at midday everything is already packed so that there is hardly any room for another 'dirndl' to find.

♦ **Tent philosophy** ♦ A tent just like one's home, where everybody knows everybody else and where you are among your own. It is just like coming home. Almost everyone is somehow related to everyone else. And if not, then one gets married to one another a few Oktoberfest seasons later.

♦ **Who comes here** ♦ Bavarian 'von' families, those with owners of names as posh as the old crayon producer Faber-Castell for example. The manageress expresses it in a simpler way: "Everything within a 50

Eduard & Claudia Reinbold

Unternehmerkinder in ihren nagelneuen Jankern vergessen, die sich noch nach der fünften Maß mit Moin, moin anbrüllen.

♦ **Besonderheit** ♦ Eigentlich ist es ja streng verboten, aber in der Schützen-Festhalle darf schon mal auf den Tischen getanzt werden. Darum tun es ab 20 Uhr praktisch alle, um sich anschließend an der Schnaps-Bar in der rechten, hinteren Zeltecke hochprozentig abzukühlen.

♦ **Die Wirte** ♦ Eddi Reinbold ist ein alter Fuchs, dem auch der „Franziskaner" gehört. Typ: Einer, der sagt, was er denkt. Frei nach Innenminister Otto Schilys Mantra: Bei mir kann jeder machen, was ich will.

♦ **Event** ♦ Am Eröffnungs-Samstag bittet das Juwelierhaus Tiffany, angeführt von Geschäftsführer Wolfi Bierlein, hundert Youngster zum „Frühstück bei Tiffany". Am letzten Wiesn-Tag werden der Landesschützenkönig und seine Königin gekürt.

kilometre radius of a Bavarian church steeple". But she forgot the business heirs from Hamburg in their brand-new 'Janker' jackets who are still shouting their Hamburg dialect "Moin, moin" at each other after their fifth litre of beer.

♦ **Special feature** ♦ Although it is strictly forbidden in the Schützen-Festhalle it is sometimes possible to dance on the tables. From eight o'clock onwards virtually everyone does it and then goes to chill out at the 'schnapps' bar in the tent's far-right corner.

♦ **The managers** ♦ Eddi Reinbold is an old hand, who also owns the restaurant Franziskaner. He does not mince his words and runs his tent according to the German home secretary Otto Schily's motto: Here, anyone can do what I want.

♦ **Event** ♦ On the first Saturday the jeweller Tiffany, run by managing director Wolfi Bierlein, invites one hundred youngsters to 'Breakfast at Tiffany's'. On the last day of the Oktoberfest this year's champion marksman and his queen are elected.

Schützen-Festhalle

Festwirte: Claudia und Eduard Reinbold
Reservierungsbüro:
T: 089-23 18 12 24, F: 089-23 18 12 44
Zeltbüro:
T: 089-50 07 74 40, F: 089-50 22 23 70
Sitzplätze: 4450
Brauerei: Löwenbräu
Musik: Die Niederalmer

Tent managers: Claudia and Eduard Reinbold
Reservations: (country code ++49)
T: (0) 89-23 18 12 24, F: (0) 89-23 18 12 44
Tent office: (country code ++49)
T: (0) 89-50 07 74 40, F: (0) 89-50 22 23 70
Seating capacity: 4,450
Brewery: Löwenbräu
Music: Die Niederalmer

Käfer's Wies'n Schänke

Käfer's Wies'n Schänke ist die Hochburg der Prominenz

♦ **Historie** ♦ Zunächst: Käfer's Wies'n Schänke ist gar kein Zelt. Sondern ein richtiges Bauernhaus, das innen wie eine gemütliche Zirbelstube wirkt. Hier fühlt man sich Zuhause. Auch deshalb geht man dorthin.

♦ **Atmosphäre** ♦ Wegen der hohen Promidichte herrscht hier ein unermüdlicher „Hey-den-kennt-man-doch"-Reflex. Man sitzt, umzingelt von bekannten Gesichtern wie Uschi Glas und Otto Waalkes, wie in einer Almhütte und schlemmt: Brotzeitbrettln mit Lachs und Salamipralinen oder die berühmt-knusprige Käfer-Ente zu Champagner in geeisten Steinkrügen. Großes Wiesnkino also, nicht ganz preiswert. Dafür darf man die handbemalten Kaffee-Haferln mit heim nehmen!

♦ **Zelt-Philosophie** ♦ Hier regieren klare Gesetze: Nur mit der richtigen Bandfarbe am Arm darf man z.B. in den ersten Stock, auf den Tanzboden. Absolutes No-No: Voyeure. Wenn Ralf Schumacher in seiner Box am Bier nippt, wird nicht plump geglotzt. Es ist normal. So fühlt sich jeder hier ganz privat und als Teil des Ganzen.

♦ **Wer hier sitzt** ♦ Unten der seriöse Gourmet – Konzernbosse, Medienmogule, Royals (Silvia v. Schweden). Oben rockt die Party- und Nachtmahl-Gesellschaft wie Elisabeth Flick, Sven Ley, die FC Bayern-Spieler (immer mittags am 2. oder 3. Wiesn-Sonntag).

Käfer's Wies'n Schänke is the tent of the glitterati

♦ **History** ♦ First of all Käfer's 'Wiesn' bar is not really a tent but a real farmhouse. Inside this house looks like a drawing room in a private home. You feel quite at home here. One of the many reasons to go there.

♦ **Atmosphere** ♦ Due to the high turn-out of celebrities a continuous 'Hey, I've-seen-him-on-telly'-reflex is ever present. You enjoy your meal surrounded by famous faces, such as actress Uschi Glas or comedian Otto Waalkes. The scenery is as if you were in a mountain hut. The food is just delicious: plowman's plate of salmon and salami-pralines or Käfer's famous crisp duck with champagne in iced stoneware jugs. Great Oktoberfest scenes, just a bit pricey. However, one may take the hand-painted coffee mugs home as a souvenir.

♦ **Tent philosophy** ♦ Clear rules apply: only those wearing the right colour ribbons on their arms are allowed onto the dance floor upstairs. An absolute no-no: nosy fans. When Ralf Schuhmacher sips his beer in his box there is no staring allowed. That is quite normal. This way everyone feels entirely private and yet still part of the whole.

♦ **Who comes here** ♦ Downstairs the serious gourmet–Germany's big company bosses, media tycoons, royalty (Silvia of Sweden). Upstairs the party people and night-time banqueteers such as Elisabeth Flick, Sven Ley, the players of Bayern Munich (always at lunch-time on the second or third Sunday) party away.

Michael Käfer

♦ **Besonderheit** ♦ Die zwei „Katzentische" à zwei Personen unter den zwei Holztreppen sind das romantischste Wiesn-Separee! Leider nur am selben Tag buchbar. Exklusiv auch: Käfers Chauffeurdienst.

♦ **Der Wirt** ♦ Den kenn ich nun wirklich gut! – und ich verrate Ihnen, Michael Käfer würde die Wiesn erfinden, wenn es sie nicht schon gäbe! Den Blick auf zehn Dinge gleichzeitig gerichtet, serviert er nicht nur Bier, sondern Abend für Abend eine Riesen Party. Ihm gehört schließlich auch der beste Club der Stadt, das P1, auch „Oanser oder Stüberl" genannt, wo nach der Wiesn weitergetanzt wird.

♦ **Events** ♦ Der „Almauftrieb" und schönste Dirndl-Laufsteg am 1. Wiesn-Sonntag. Der Stammtisch eines Verlags-Erben aus New York. Dabei: ein Strumpf-Fabrikant, ein Prinz, ein Bankier, ein Landwirt, ein Versand-König, ein Jet-Setter. Und die „Charity-Käfer Kinderwiesn" am 1. Wiesn-Dienstag.

♦ **Special feature** ♦ Two tiny tables, each for two people, beneath the two timber staircases, the most romantic Oktoberfest booth. They can be reserved, but only on the same day. The chauffeur service is also exclusive.

♦ **The manager** ♦ Now, him I know really very well!–and from personal experience I can tell you Michael Käfer would invent the Oktoberfest if it did not already exist! Always doing ten things at the same time, he not only serves beer, but each and every evening he throws an enormous party. The best club in town also belongs to him, the 'P1', a.k.a. 'Oanser' (number one) or 'Stüberl' (front room), where you can continue to party after the Oktoberfest tents are closed.

♦ **Events** ♦ The 'Almauftrieb' and prettiest 'dirndl' competition on the first Sunday. The regular get-together of a publishing house heir from New York, including a sock manufacturer, a prince, a banker, a farmer, a mail-order tycoon, a jet setter. And there is also the charity Käfer children's Oktoberfest on the first Tuesday.

Käfer's Wies'n Schänke

Festwirt: Michael Käfer
Reservierungsbüro:
T: 089-41 68 356, F: 089-41 68 880
Zeltbüro:
T: 089-50 07 73 34, F: 089-50 07 74 47
Sitzplätze: 3000
Brauerei: Paulaner
Musik: Gary & Gerry, Dreirad, California Sun
www.feinkost-kaefer.de

Tent manager: Michael Käfer
Reservations: (country code ++49)
T: (0) 89-41 68 356, F: (0) 89-41 68 880
Tent office: (country code ++49)
T: (0) 89-50 07 73 34, F: (0) 89-50 07 74 47
Seating capacity: 3,000
Brewery: Paulaner
Music: Gary & Gerry, Dreirad, California Sun
www.feinkost-kaefer.de

Weinzelt

Das Weinzelt macht lustig ...

♦ **Historie** ♦ Wein wurde schon immer ausgeschenkt auf dem Münchner Oktoberfest. Das reine Weinzelt mit seiner prickelnden Sektbar jedoch gibt es erst seit 1984.

♦ **Atmosphäre** ♦ Hier werden Ohren und Gaumen angeregt: Die drei Bands, die Blechblos'n, die Sumpfkröten und die Högl Fun Band sind Kult. Je mehr Champagner auf die Bühne zu den Musikern gereicht wird, desto fetziger spielen sie. Zu „Anton aus Tirol" gibt es dann alles, was zum Wein passt: Schwäbischen Zwiebelkuchen oder Pfälzer Leberknödel mit Sauerkraut.

♦ **Zelt-Philosophie** ♦ Im Weinzelt nach einer Maß zu fragen, wäre ungefähr so, wie wenn Sie von einem Bayerischen Bäcker ein Brötchen kaufen wollten. Man versteht Sie nicht. Im Weinzelt trinkt natürlich alles Wein und Sekt oder allerhöchstens Weißbier. Wer also absolut kein Bier mag, der kann hier trotzdem fröhlich werden.

♦ **Wer hier sitzt** ♦ Hinterm Tresen: alle guten Jahrgänge. Vor der Theke: das Apres-Ski-Publikum aus Kitzbühel und Münchens umliegenden schicken Tälern. Hanseaten, die gern vor ihrer Schorle sitzen. Italiener natürlich. Und alle feinen Leute, denen der 1-Liter-Bierkrug einfach zu schwer zu heben ist.

The wine tent makes you merry ...

♦ **History** ♦ Wine has always been served at the Munich Oktoberfest. An only wine-serving tent with its sparkling-wine bar, however, was only established in 1984.

♦ **Atmosphere** ♦ Your ears and your taste buds are both stimulated here: The three bands, the Sumpfkröten, Blechblosn and the Högl Fun Band, enjoy cult status. The more champagne is passed to the musicians on stage, the faster and louder they play. During a typical favourite 'Anton aus Tirol' you may eat anything that goes well with wine: Swabian quiche or Palatine liver dumpling with 'sauerkraut'.

♦ **Tent philosophy** ♦ Asking for beer in the wine tent would be like asking a Bavarian baker for muffins. He would not understand. In the wine tent the only drink is wine or champagne, perhaps a wheat beer at the very most. In this tent those who absolutely do not drink beer can enjoy themselves as much as the rest.

♦ **Who comes here** ♦ Behind the bar: every good vintage. In front: the après-ski crowd from Kitzbühl or from Munich's hip surrounding valleys. Hamburg citizens, happy to sit in front of their spritzers. Italians of course and the posh people who quite simply cannot lift a one-litre beer mug to save their life.

Doris & Roland Kuffler

♦ **Besonderheit** ♦ Das Weinzelt ist berühmt für hervorragende Tropfen, hier wird kein „Chateaux Migräne" ausgeschenkt. Genauso gut spielt die Musik. Wer dann immer noch keine roten Bäckchen hat, sollte mal den heißen Flammkuchen probieren.

♦ **Die Wirte** ♦ Roland Kuffler gehört nicht nur das Seehaus und das Spatenhaus an der Oper. Zu ihm gehört auch Frau Doris, die immer die schönsten Dirndl trägt.

♦ **Event** ♦ „Sex and the City" life erlebt man täglich an der Sektbar, wenn sich dort die geheimen Frauenstammtische und Mädels-Abende zusammenfinden ...

♦ **Special feature** ♦ The wine tent is famous for its great selection of wines. You will not find a 'Chateau Migraine' here. The music is equally good and if the colour still has not risen to your face you should try the Flammkuchen (tarte flambé), served while hot.

♦ **The managers** ♦ Roland Kuffler owns the Seehaus restaurant and the Spatenhaus by the Munich opera house as well and his wife Doris always wears the prettiest 'dirndl'.

♦ **Event** ♦ You can experience 'Sex and the City' live at the sparkling-wine bar where women meet up for a girls' night out.

Weinzelt

Festwirte:
Roland, Doris und Stephan Kuffler
Reservierungsbüro:
T: 089-29 07 05 17, F: 089-24 24 38 81
Zeltbüro:
T: 089-50 07 74 11, F: 089-50 22 23 62
Sitzplätze: 2500
Musik: Die Sumpfkröten, Blechblos'n, Högl Fun Band
www.kuffler-gastronomie.de

Tent managers:
Roland, Doris and Stephan Kuffler
Reservations: (country code ++49)
T: (0) 89-29 07 05 17, F: (0) 89-24 24 38 81
Tent office: (country code ++49)
T: (0) 89-50 07 74 11, F: (0) 89-50 22 23 62
Seating capacity: 2,500
Music: Die Sumpfkröten, Blechblosn, Högl Fun Band
www.kuffler-gastronomie.de

Löwenbräu-Festhalle

In der Löwenbräu-Festhalle kocht die Stimmung über

♦ **Historie** ♦ Meteorologen nach bräuchte die Wiesn eigentlich einen eigenen Wetterbericht. Auf der kann es in den Abendstunden nämlich um 10 Grad wärmer sein als in der Münchner City. Auch – oder vor allem – weil es das Löwenbräu gibt!

♦ **Atmosphäre** ♦ Vorm Eingang schwenkt ein Riesenlöwe einen Bierkrug und brüllt immerzu: Löwenbräu. Drinnen tobt das Volk. Und ab 18 Uhr fiedelt Heinz auf seiner E-Geige wie Robbie Williams, dass die Krüge springen. In einem Jahr lagen 26 Tonnen Glasscherben von 36 000 Krügen auf dem Zeltboden. Mehr muss man wohl nicht sagen.

♦ **Zelt-Philosophie** ♦ Hier regiert ein klares Konzept: Alle sind gleich, will die Riesenbierhalle dem Gast sagen. Unterschiede? Gibt es nicht. Die Studentin und der Künstler, der Italiener neben dem Franzosen – alle sollen sich gleich wohl fühlen. Tun sie auch. Das Löwenbräu ist wie völkerverbindender Biergarten.

♦ **Wer hier sitzt** ♦ „Da samma wieder", sagt man im Löwenbräu. Hier sitzen von Freitag bis Sonntag jedes Jahr die gleichen Firmen, Münchner und Alt-Popper in den gleichen Krachledernen an den gleichen Tischen und werden von den gleichen Kellnerinnen bedient. So will man's hier, so soll es bleiben. Nur an den Wochenenden wird Platz gemacht für die Italiener, die das Exportbier auch sehr schätzen.

In the Löwenbräu-Festhalle the emotions boil over

♦ **History** ♦ According to meteorologists the Oktoberfest would need its own weather forecast. Here it can be up to ten degrees warmer during the evening hours than in the city centre, also–or mainly because–there is the Löwenbräu tent!

♦ **Atmosphere** ♦ At the entrance a giant lion waves a beer mug and roars constantly: Löwenbräu. Inside the tent people are partying from 6 pm onwards, Heinz plays his electric violin like a pop star and keeps the beer mugs dancing. In one year over 28 tons of glass from 36,000 smashed mugs littered the floor of the beer tent. Say no more ...

♦ **Tent philosophy** ♦ One clear message: The giant beer tent suggests to its visitors that everyone is equal. Differences? Do not exist. The student and the artist, the Italian next to the Frenchman–all should feel equally at ease. And they do. The Löwenbräu tent is like a beer garden, bringing people together.

♦ **Who comes here** ♦ "Here we are again", one says in the Löwenbräu tent. Every year the same companies are here from Friday to Sunday, Munich citizens in the same 'lederhosen' at the same tables and served by the same waitresses. And that is just the way they like it, that is how it should stay. Only at weekends they make room for the Italians who also appreciate the export beer.

Ludwig Hagn & Stephanie Spendler

♦ **Besonderheit** ♦ Jeden Nachmittag um fünf spielt Kapellmeister Hans Meier die Hymne „Amazing Grace" mit vier Trompetern auf der Empore, direkt am Fenster, durch das dann die rote Abendsonne scheint (– nein, keine Attrappe!!!). Dann ist das ganze Zelt still ...

♦ **Die Wirte** ♦ Urgestein Wiggerl Hagn ist bodenständig mit Herz und Bauch. Er ist der Wiesnwirt mit der längsten Dienstzeit und der Präsident vom Bayerischen Hotel- und Gaststättenverband. Einer, der seine 160 Mitarbeiter alle beim Namen kennt. Ein echter Wiesn-Papa.

♦ **Event** ♦ Jeden Morgen um 8 Uhr frühstückt der Wirt mit seinem Personal. Da sieht man die Wiesn im Aufbruch.

♦ **Special feature** ♦ Every afternoon at five the band leader Hans Meier plays the hymn "Amazing Grace" with four trumpeters up in the gallery, standing directly at the window, through which the red evening sunlight comes in (no, it is not a fake!). The whole tent goes very quiet ...

♦ **The managers** ♦ Wiggerl Hagn is down to earth, with his heart and belly. He is the longest-serving tent manager and also president of the Bavarian Hotel, Bar and Restaurant association. He is one of those who know all their 160 employees by name, a real Oktoberfest papa.

♦ **Event** ♦ Every morning at eight o'clock the manager has breakfast with his staff. A good example of the Oktoberfest getting ready for another day.

Löwenbräu-Festhalle

Festwirte:
Ludwig Hagn und Stephanie Spendler
Reservierungsbüro:
T: 089-47 76 77, F: 089-470 58 48
Zeltbüro:
T: 089-50 07 75 30, F: 089-50 07 75 24
Sitzplätze: 8500
Brauerei: Löwenbräu
Musik: Bert Hansmaiers Heldensteiner
www.loewenbraeu-festzelt.info

Tent managers:
Ludwig Hagn and Stephanie Spendler
Reservations: (country code ++49)
T: (0) 89-47 76 77, F: (0) 89-470 58 48
Tent office: (country code ++49)
T: 089-50 07 75 30, F: 089-50 07 75 24
Seating capacity: 8,500
Brewery: Löwenbräu
Music: Bert Hansmaiers Heldensteiner
www.loewenbraeu-festzelt.info

Kas und Wurst
Haxn u. Enten
Spanferkel

Löwenbräu-Festhalle

Bräurosl

In der Bräurosl feiert alles, was das Leben so anspült

♦ **Historie** ♦ Die Bräurosl ist ohne jeden Schnörkel. Zwei Maibäume sind das Wahrzeichen vor der Tür. Seinen Namen hat das Zelt nach der Tochter eines Brauereibesitzers. Die Bräurosl ist jeden Abend auf ihrem Pferd durch den Brauereihof geritten, wobei sie sich ihren Abend-Schoppen gönnte.

♦ **Atmosphäre** ♦ Die Bräurosl ist wie es klingt: Herzig, gemütlich, komisch, süffig, bayerisch. Hinter jeder Maß steckt meist ein uriger Kopf, dem der Gesang der Bräurosljodlerin genauso schmeckt wie das Spanferkel in der Festbiersoße.

♦ **Zelt-Philosophie** ♦ Ein Besuch ist wie ein buntes Familienfest rund um den Maibaum. Alles singt und lacht. Nur die Hubertus-Box bleibt ein Privileg.

Wer dort rein darf, bestimmt die Wirtin. Sie überwacht auch das Design für den Wiesnsammlersteinbierkrug, den es jedes Jahr neu zum Sammeln gibt.

♦ **Wer hier sitzt** ♦ Hier hockt, was das Leben so anspült: der Klempner, die Pastorenfamilie, Spieler und Fußballfans der „Löwen 1860". Sowie die Menschen von den „bayerischen Meeren": dem Ammersee, dem Starnbergersee. „Heut gemma in die Bräurosl", sagen die nach dem Golfen. Die ist ein äußerst liberales Zelt. Fällt hier einer mal von der Bank, ist das auch okay. „Des koa scho ma passiern", sagt die Wirtin. „Mir san geländegängig."

Just about everyone from life's rich palette parties in the Bräurosl tent

♦ **History** ♦ Bräurosl is without any frills. The two maypoles in front of the main entrance are its characteristic emblem. The tent has its name from a brewery owner's daughter. Every evening the Bräurosl (brewer's Rosie) rode through the brewer's yard on her horse and would stop there for a pint of beer.

♦ **Atmosphere** ♦ Bräurosl is rather like the name suggests: warm, comfy, funny, rich in flavour, Bavarian. Sitting behind each mug you will find a typical local who enjoys the yodelling of the Bräurosl singer just as much as the pork with beer gravy.

♦ **Tent philosophy** ♦ A visit to this tent is like a colourful family celebration around the maypole. Everyone sings and laughs. Only the Hubertus box remains a privilege. The manageress decides who is allowed in. She also supervises the design for the Oktoberfest collectors' beer stein which is issued anew every year.

♦ **Who comes here** ♦ Here you will find people from all walks of life sitting happily together: the plumber, the pastor's family, footballers and fans of another football club, the 'Munich Lions 1860'. Additionally the people from around the 'Bavarian seas': from the Ammer and Starnberger lakes. "Today we'll go to Bräurosl", they say after a round of golf. Bräurosl is an extremely liberal tent. If someone falls off the bench, that is ok, too. "That can happen", the landlady says, "We'll take it as it comes."

Renate & Georg Heide

♦ Besonderheit ♦ Der Senior, Willy Heide, pilgert jedes Jahr vor der Wiesn von Planegg in den Wallfahrtsort Maria Eich. Dort zündet er seit zwölf Jahren eine Kerze an, und bittet um eine friedliche Wiesn.

♦ Die Wirte ♦ Sind wie die Atmosphäre. Seit 66 Jahren ist die Bräurosl in den Händen derselben Familie. Anpacken lautet deren Devise. Dazu gehört, dass die Bedienungen lernen, 14 Krüge – rund 14 Kilo – auf einmal zu tragen.

♦ Events ♦ Immer am ersten Wiesn-Sonntag trifft sich hier die „Schwulen-Community". Und jedes Jahr lädt Wirte-Senior Willy Heide alle Wirte zu seinem kulinarisch gefürchteten Kalbsbriesmilzwurstessen. Am letzten Wiesntag wird hier die offizielle Verabschiedung des Personals mit Goaßlschnalzern und anderen Künstlern festlich zelebriert (20 bis 22 Uhr).

♦ Special feature ♦ The senior manager, Willy Heide, goes on a pilgrimage from Planegg to Maria Eich each year before the Oktoberfest. He lights a candle, as he has done for the last twelve years, and prays for a peaceful 'Wiesn'.

♦ The managers ♦ Are like the atmosphere. Bräurosl has been in the hands of the same family for sixty-six years. They are a very hands-on family. That the waitresses have to learn to carry as many as 14 beer mugs–over thirty pounds–is all part of it.

♦ Event ♦ Always on the first Sunday the gay and lesbian community meets here. Each year the senior manager Willy Heide invites all the beer tent managers to his much-feared culinary speciality, sausages made with calves' spleen. On the last day of the Oktoberfest the official farewell to the personnel is celebrated with Goaßlschnalzern (coachmen's whip lashing) and other artistes (8–10 pm).

Bräurosl

Festwirte: Renate und Georg Heide
Reservierungsbüro:
T: 089-89 55 63 53, F: 089-89 55 63 56
Zeltbüro:
T: (0) 89-50 07 75 60, F: (0) 89-50 07 75 74
Sitzplätze: 8400
Brauerei: Hacker-Pschorr
Musik: Ludwig Thoma-Musikanten, Südtiroler Spitzbuam

Tent managers: Renate and Georg Heide
Reservations: (country code ++49)
T: (0) 89-89 55 63 53, F: (0) 89-89 55 63 56
Tent office: (country code ++49)
T: (0) 89-50 07 75 60, F: (0) 89-50 07 75 74
Seating capacity: 8,400
Brewery: Hacker-Pschorr
Music: Ludwig Thoma Musikanten, Südtiroler Spitzbuam

Augustiner-Festhalle

Die Augustiner-Festhalle ist berühmt für das älteste Bier

♦ **Historie** ♦ 1328 ist eine wichtige Jahreszahl, die Münchner Kindl schon im Heimat- und Sachkunde-Unterricht an der Grundschule lernen. Da wurde nämlich aus Münchner Sicht eines der besten Biere der Welt gebraut – und zwar von Mönchen einst, wie die meisten anderen Biere auch.

♦ **Atmosphäre** ♦ In der Augustiner-Festhalle fühlt sich der zu Hause, der mag, was er auch kennt. Und es liebt, wie in einem Holzfass zu sitzen, so schön dunkel, deutsch. Hier lebt noch Wiesn-Nostalgie.

♦ **Zelt-Philosophie** ♦ Mir san mir und das reicht uns. Die Augustiner-Festhalle ist authentisch. Ein Zelt wie ein großer Stammtisch, bei dem Boxen-Plätze sogar vererbt werden können.

♦ **Wer hier sitzt** ♦ Altplayboy Gunter Sachs, wenn die St.Tropez-Saison beendet ist. Die reellen Reichen: Der Münchner Villenbesitzer. Nicht zu verwechseln mit dem Immobilienhai – der hockt an der Bar des Hippodroms. Familien mit Kindern. Die Tegernseer Stammtische.

♦ **Besonderheit** ♦ Das 1200 Gramm große Hendl, mit Petersilie gewürzt und Butter bestrichen.

♦ **Der Wirt** ♦ Nein, bayerisch heißt nicht immer nur Rumm-ta-ta. Manfred Vollmer wirkt zurückhaltend.

The Augustiner-Festhalle is famous for the oldest beer

♦ **History** ♦ 1328 is an important year that Munich kids already learn about in their general knowledge and local history lessons in primary school. In that year, according to the locals, one of the best beers in the world was brewed—by monks in those days, like most other beers, too.

♦ **Atmosphere** ♦ The beer drinker who likes what he already knows feels quite at home in the Augustiner-Festhalle. It is wonderful to be here, like sitting in a wooden barrel, so dark, so German. Here Oktoberfest nostalgia is very much alive.

♦ **Tent philosophy** ♦ "We know who we are and that is good enough for us". The Augustiner-Festhalle is authentic. A beer tent like one big table, where regular seating rights in the boxes can even be inherited.

♦ **Who comes here** ♦ The old playboy Gunter Sachs, when the St. Tropez season comes to an end. The really rich: The Munich villa owner. Not to be confused with the property developer—he sits at the bar in the Hippodrom. Families with children. The regulars from the Tegernsee region.

♦ **Special feature** ♦ The large—over two pound—grilled chicken, seasoned with parsley and daubed with butter.

Manfred Vollmer

Dabei dirigieren seine Augen das Personal wie ein Orchester. Und das spielt grandios.

♦ **Events** ♦ Das Erlebnis im Augustiner ist im Grunde jede Maß Bier. Das Bier auf dem Oktoberfest wird aus stählernen Drucktanks ausgeschenkt. Nur im Augustiner wird es noch aus Holzfässern, sogenannten „Hirschen", gezapft, die mindestens 200 Liter Fassungsvermögen besitzen.

♦ **The manager** ♦ Bavarian does not always mean only Oom-pa-pa. Manfred Vollmer appears reserved, although his eyes conduct his personnel like an orchestra, and it plays magnificently.

♦ **Events** ♦The great experience in the Augustiner tent is basically every single mug of beer. The other beers here at the Oktoberfest are served from high-pressure steel tanks. Only in the Augustiner tent is it tapped from wooden barrels, the so-called 'hirschen', which have at least 200 litres capacity.

Augustiner-Festhalle

Festwirt: Manfred Vollmer
Reservierungsbüro:
T: 089-23 18 32 66, F: 089-2 60 53 79
Zeltbüro:
T: 089-50 07 74 70, F: 089-50 07 74 71
Sitzplätze: 8500
Brauerei: Augustiner-Bräu
Musik: Blaskapelle Reinhard Hagitte

Tent manager: Manfred Vollmer
Reservations: (country code ++49)
T: (0) 89-23 18 32 66, F: (0) 89-2 60 53 79
Tent office: (country code ++49)
T: (0) 89-50 07 74 70, F: (0) 89-50 07 74 71
Seating capacity: 8,500
Brewery: Augustiner-Bräu
Music: Blaskapelle Reinhard Hagitte

Augustiner-Festhalle

Ochsenbraterei

In der Ochsenbraterei beginnt der Wiesntag

♦ **Historie** ♦ Das Macho-Zelt. Hier dreht sich alles um den Ochsen. Rund 90 Stück werden hier pro Wiesn verputzt.

♦ **Atmosphäre** ♦ Kein Wunder, dass dieses Zelt überkocht, wenn schon morgens die Herde voll hochgedreht werden. In die Ochsenbraterei geht man nämlich schon zum Frühschoppen. Rund 450 Kilo wiegt übrigens ein Ochse, der sich hier am Spieß dreht.

♦ **Zelt-Philosophie** ♦ In der Ochsenbraterei geht es nicht um Äußerlichkeiten. Wer kommt, was man trägt, ist hier egal. Das Auge richtet sich nur auf eins: den Ochsen. Und natürlich auf das Bier. Aber werden Sie bitte nicht sentimental. Jeder Ochse hat nämlich einen Namen. Da grillt dann also Fridolin, Franz oder Rudolph vor Ihnen, bevor er Ihnen in Scheibchen zerlegt und mit warmem Kartoffelsalat serviert wird.

♦ **Wer hier sitzt** ♦ Die Ochsenbraterei ist die gute Stube der Einheimischen. Hier sitzen die Münchner und ihre Familien, vor allem Sonntagmittags. Wochentags gehört die Ochsenbraterei den Stammtischvätern.

♦ **Besonderheit** ♦ Die Ochsenbraterei ist das beliebteste Mittagszelt, vor allem unter der Woche. Und noch besser an den Dienstagen. Dann gibt es nämlich, wie überhaupt auf der ganzen Wiesn, ermäßigte Preise.

In the Ochsenbraterei the 'Wiesn' day begins

♦ **History** ♦ The Ochsenbraterei (roasted-ox stall) is the macho tent where everything revolves around the oxen. About ninety are eaten during one Oktoberfest.

♦ **Atmosphere** ♦ It is no wonder that this tent overheats, when already in the morning the heat of the huge rotisseries is turned up. Some guests come here for their morning drinks. Incidentally the oxen turning on the spits here weigh not much less than a thousand pounds.

♦ **Tent philosophy** ♦ Outward appearances are unimportant in the Ochsenbraterei. Who comes and what they wear does not matter. All eyes are looking only at one thing and that is the oxen. Yes, of course, at the beer as well. However, please do not get sentimental: Each ox has a name. Before your very eyes Fridolin, Franz or Rudolph is being grilled, before he is cut into slices and served with warm potato salad.

♦ **Who comes here** ♦ The Ochsenbraterei is like a drawing room to the natives. Munich families sit here mainly at Sunday lunchtime. On weekdays the oxen grill belongs to the 'regulars' at their usual tables.

♦ **Special feature** ♦ It is the favourite lunchtime tent, especially during the week and even more so on Tuesdays, since that means reduced prices all over the Oktoberfest.

Anneliese & Hermann Haberl

♦ **Die Wirte** ♦ Anneliese und Hermann Haberl drehen nicht nur den Spieß, sondern in München ein großes Rad: Sie betreiben zum Beispiel den berühmten Biergarten am Chinesischen Turm im Englischen Garten, sowie die Gastronomie auf dem Olympiagelände.

♦ **Events** ♦ Immer in der zweiten Wiesnwoche treffen sich hier alle Wiesnwirte morgens um elf, hinten in der Hausbox zum Ochsenbraten und sinnieren über die Wiesn-Halbzeit. Und am letzten Wiesn-Abend bläst der Wiesnwirt auf seiner Trompete das Abschiedslied.

♦ **The manager** ♦ Anneliese and Hermann Haberl not only turn the spits, they also operate many other things around town. They run for instance the famous beer garden at the Chinesischer Turm (Chinese tower) in the park knows as Englischer Garten, as well as the eateries in the Olympia park.

♦ **Events** ♦ During the second week of the Oktoberfest all the tent managers meet here for roast oxen at 11 am in the house box at the back of the tent. Halfway through the 'Wiesn' they talk about events so far. On the final evening of the Oktoberfest the beer tent manager plays a farewell song on his trumpet.

Ochsenbraterei

Festwirte: Anneliese und Hermann Haberl, Antje Schneider
Reservierungsbüro:
T: 089-38 38 73 12, F: 089-38 38 73 40
Zeltbüro:
T: 089-51 11 58 0, F: 089-51 11 58 10
Sitzplätze: 7400
Brauerei: Spatenbräu
Musik: Bruno Gress Blasmusik, SAX'N'DI Band
www.ochsenbraterei.de

Tent managers: Anneliese and Hermann Haberl, Antje Schneider
Reservations: (country code ++49)
T: (0) 89-38 38 73 12, F: (0) 89-38 38 73 40
Tent office: (country code ++49)
T: (0) 89-51 11 58 0, F: (0) 89-51 11 58 10
Seating capacity: 7,400
Brewery: Spatenbräu
Music: Bruno Gress Blasmusik, SAX'N'DI Band
www.ochsenbraterei.de

Fischer-Vroni

In der Fischer-Vroni gibt's den beliebten Steckerlfisch

♦ **Historie** ♦ Die Fischer-Vroni ist das erste Zelt am Eingang zur Wirtsbudenstraße, und hat schon deshalb so viele Besucher, weil man quasi in sie hineinstolpert.

♦ **Atmosphäre** ♦ Wenn man durch ihre Türe tritt, hat man das Wörtchen „Räucherküche" im Kopf: Und ein gedankliches Rendezvous mit Fischers Fritze am Lagerfeuer. Öffnet man die Augen wieder, steht man auch hier in einem ganz normalen Bierzelt. Einziger Unterschied: Hier wird in erster Linie frischer Fisch serviert.

♦ **Zelt-Philosophie** ♦ Die Fischer-Vroni ist so unspektakulär, dass sie schon wieder spektakulär ist.

♦ **Wer hier sitzt** ♦ Hier kommt jeder mal vorbei: Münchner Serienstars wie Wolfi Vierek und Jutta Speidel. Angler und Vegetarier. Und freitags, am Fischttag, der Katholik.

♦ **Besonderheit** ♦ Der Steckerlfisch ist die große Wiesnspezialität seit 1952: Zander, Makrele und Lachsforelle werden auf einem Stock aufgespießt und in einer 15 Meter langen Reihe über offenem Feuer vor dem Zelt gegrillt. Fischer können sogar ihren eigenen Fischfang mitbringen und gegen ein Trinkgeld über dem Bodenfeuer am Steckerl räuchern.

At Fischer Vroni they serve the much-loved 'Steckerlfisch'

♦ **History** ♦ Fischer Vroni is the first tent at the entrance to the Wirtsbudenstraße (food stall lane). It has so many visitors due to its prominent position they just seem to wander in.

♦ **Atmosphere** ♦ When you step through the door, your first impression is of a smoke room and you imagine a rendezvous with fishermen at their camp fire. Open your eyes again and you are standing in a perfectly ordinary beer tent. The only difference is that mainly fresh fish is served.

♦ **Tent philosophy** ♦ The Fischer Vroni tent is so unobtrusive that it quickly becomes very noticeable.

♦ **Who comes here** ♦ Everybody comes by every now and then. Munich TV stars like Wolfi Vierek and Jutta Speidel; anglers and vegetarians too and on Fridays, their fish-only day, the Catholics.

♦ **Special feature** ♦ 'Steckerlfisch' (smoked fish) has been the great Oktoberfest speciality since 1952: zander, mackerel and salmon-trout are skewered on a stick ('steckerl') and in a fifty-foot long row grilled on an open fire in front of the tent. Fishermen can even bring along their own catch and, for a small tip, smoke their skewered fish over the open fire.

♦ **Der Wirt** ♦ Die zwei quirligen Schwestern Eva und Anita waren einst die berühmten Fischer Vronis. Heute führt Hans Stadtmüller als jüngster Wiesn-Wirt das Zelt für die verstorbene Mutter und Tante weiter.

♦ **Events** ♦ Jeden zweiten Wiesn-Montag treffen sich hier aus ganz Deutschland rund 1200 geschlechtlich Gleichgesinnte ab 14 Uhr (Info: www.rosawiesn.de). Und dann tritt Lady Bubbles, ein Transvestit, als Marlene Dietrich verkleidet auf.

♦ **The manager** ♦ The two lively sisters Eva and Anita were once the famous Fischer Vronis. Today Hans Stadtmüller, the youngest tent manager at the Oktoberfest, continues to run the tent, replacing his late mother and aunt.

♦ **Events** ♦ Each year, on the second Monday, around 1,200 gays and lesbians from all over Germany meet here at 2 pm (information: www.rosawiesn.de). There is also a routine from transvestite Lady Bubbles, dressed as Marlene Dietrich.

Fischer-Vroni

Festwirt: Johann Stadtmüller
Reservierungsbüro:
T: 089-66 10 42, F: 089-65 25 34
Zeltbüro:
T: 089-50 07 72 20, F: 089-50 07 73 20
Sitzplätze: 3430
Brauerei: Augustiner-Bräu
Musik: Sepp Folger und seine Münchner Musikanten
www.fischer-vroni.de

Tent manager: Johann Stadtmüller
Reservations: (country code ++49)
T: (0) 89-66 10 42, F: (0) 89-65 25 34
Tent office: (country code ++49)
T: 089-50 07 72 20, F: 089-50 07 73 20
Seating capacity: 3,430
Brewery: Augustiner-Bräu
Music: Sepp Folger and his Münchner Musikanten
www.fischer-vroni.de

Hendl-Rezept

Das Brathendl fast wie auf der Wiesn

(von Andreas Geitl, Küchenchef vom Winzerer Fähndl)

Mancher gibt sich viele Müh,
mit dem lieben Federvieh;
Einesteils der Eier wegen,
welche diese Vögel legen;
Zweitens: Weil man dann und wann
einen Braten essen kann ...

(Wilhelm Busch, Max und Moritz, Erster Streich)

Roast chicken recipe

Roast chicken almost the same as at the Oktoberfest

(by Andreas Geitl, chef at Winzerer Fähndl)

I'd say my chicken's lot is fate,
When thought of in its slaughtered state,
But eggs galore to boil and fry,
Can I this sweet fowl's life deny?
Though, try resist the thought of it:
That fattened chicken on the spit ...

Und hier ist das Wiesn-Rezept dazu!

Für zwei Personen brauchen Sie:

- **1 frisches 1200 g Brathendl (Wichtig: Trockenschlachtung!)**
- **Salz und Pfeffer**
- **Reichlich frische Blattpetersilie mit Stängel**
- **50 Gramm ungesalzene Butter**

Und so gelingt es:

Das Brathendl ca. eine Stunde vor dem Braten von innen und außen richtig kräftig mit Pfeffer und Salz würzen, so dass man schon vom Zubereiten Durst bekommt.

Den Bauch mit grob zerkleinerter, gewaschener und noch feuchter Petersilie füllen. Wenn Sie zusätzliche Feuchtigkeit

And here is the Oktoberfest recipe!

For two people, you will need

- **A fresh 2lb. 10oz. (1,200g) chicken (important: dry-plucked)**
- **Salt and pepper**
- **Ample fresh leaf-parsley with stalks**
- **1 3/4 oz. (50g) unsalted butter**

And here is how it is done:

About 1 hour before roasting, season the chicken inside and out with quite a lot of pepper and salt, so that even the preparation makes your mouth water.

Stuff the bird with the roughly chopped, washed and still wet parsley. With this added moisture inside, the chicken remains juicy and the parsley leaves can give off more of their aroma.

in den Bauch bringen, bleibt das Hendl saftiger und die Petersilie kann mehr Aroma abgeben.
Sollten Sie einen Drehgrill besitzen, spießen Sie das Hendl auf und grillen Sie es bei etwa 220° ca. eine Stunde. Ansonsten lässt sich das Wiesnhendl auch in einem passenden Bräter zubereiten, den Sie zuvor mit etwas Fett ausstreichen.
Das Hendl zunächst mit der Brustseite nach unten einlegen und in den auf 200° vorgeheizten Ofen schieben. Bitte keine Heißluft verwenden. Durch die ständige Luftzirkulation wird das Hendl zwar gleichmäßiger braun aber auch trocken. Nach etwa 30 Minuten wenden und mit der Brustseite nach oben fertig braten. Man rechnet ca. 1 Stunde Bratzeit pro Kilogramm.
Etwa 15 Minuten vor Ende der Garzeit wird das Hendl mit frischer, weicher, jedoch nicht flüssiger Butter bepinselt. Vorgang vier- bis fünfmal wiederholen.
Das Hendl ist gar, wenn klarer Saft aus dem Bauchraum läuft.

Should you have a rotating grill, skewer the chicken and roast it at about 220° for about an hour. Alternatively the Oktoberfest chicken can also be prepared in an suitable, greased roasting dish.
The bird should then be placed breast down in the dish and put into the oven, preheated to 200°. Do not use the fan, otherwise the continuous circulation of air will colour the chicken evenly but will also dry it out.
Turn the bird around after about 30 minutes and the chicken finishes roasting its breast facing upward. It will need approximately 25 minutes roasting per pound (1 hour/kg).
About fifteen minutes before the end of the cooking time, the bird should be coated with fresh, soft but not runny butter. Repeat this process four to five times.
The chicken is ready when clear juice comes out.

Bis zu 10 000 Menschen sitzen in einem großen Bierzelt. Waaas? Wie bitte?! Das ist Ihnen zu laut, haben Sie gesagt? Okay, aber deshalb müssen Sie ja nicht gleich ganz auf das Oktoberfest verzichten. Weichen Sie einfach in eines der 50 kleineren Zelte oder Imbissbuden aus. **Meine 4 Lieblinge unter den Mini-Zelten:**

Münchner Knödelei

Festwirte:
Bettina und Florian Oberndorfer
Reservierungsbüro:
T: 089-4 48 14 00, F: 089-82 02 07 43
Sitzplätze: 390
www.muenchner-knoedelei.de

Proprietors:
Bettina and Florian Oberndorfer
Reservations: (country code ++49)
T: (0)89-4 48 14 00, F: (0)89-82 02 07 43
Seating capacity: 390
www.muenchner-knoedelei.de

Die Münchner Knödelei liegt zwischen Geisterbahn und Riesenrad in der Straße 5 und sieht von außen aus wie ein Puppenherd mit einer Riesen-Suppenkelle, die vom Dach hängt. Auch innen ist alles puppenstubenklein mit dunklen Holzbänken vor dunklen Holztischen und einer Wirtin wie Schneewittchen, die jeden Ihrer Gäste persönlich begrüßt. Ab dann dreht sich alles nur noch um den Knödel. Über 50 verschiedene Sorten rollen hier vom Teller in die Bäuche: Semmelknödel, Kartoffelknödel, Steinpilzknödel, der rustikale Bergkas, der Rote-Beete- und Spinatknödel, Fleischknödel, aber auch süße Topfenknödel. Sie sind eine hervorragende Grundlage fürs Bier, und schmecken besonders auch den kleinen Besuchern.

The Münchner Knödelei (dumpling shop) is situated between the ghost train and the Ferris wheel in street # 5. From the outside it looks like a doll-house stove with a giant ladle hanging from the roof. Inside everything is minuscule as well, with dark wooden benches around dark wooden tables and a manageress who looks like Snow White and greets all her guests in person. Once you are settled, everything revolves around the 'knödel'. Over fifty varieties make their way from the plates to the bellies. The different varieties include main ingredients such as bread rolls, potatoes, mushrooms, rustic cheeses, beetroot and spinach, or meat. They can also be sweet rather than savoury: made with quark or frommage frais. They line your stomach perfectly for the beer and the kids love them.

Up to 10,000 people fit into one of the big beer tents. Whaaat? What did you say?! That's too noisy, I hear you say. All right then, but that is no reason to completely forgo the pleasures of the Oktoberfest. Visit one of the fifty smaller tents or food stalls instead. **My four favourite places among the mini beer tents are:**

Bodo's Backstube

Festwirt: Bodo E. Müller
Reservierungsbüro:
T: 089-2 36 65 20, F: 089-26 36 00
Zeltbüro:
T: 089-50 22 22 33, F: 089-50 22 22 43
Sitzplätze: 450
www.bodos.de

Proprietor: Bodo E. Müller
Reservations: (country code ++49)
T: (0)89-2 36 65 20, F: (0)89-26 36 00
Tent office: (country code ++49)
T: (0)89- 50 22 22 33, F: (0)89- 50 22 22 43
Seating capacity: 450
www.bodos.de

Die schrille Backstube zwischen Ochsenbraterei und Augustiner-Festhalle in der Straße 2 ist ein Wiesn-Klassiker, dekoriert mit Amor-Engeln auf plüschigen Wolken, die von der Decke hängen. Und wer aufs Häusl muss, den lächeln bekannte Gesichter wie Lothar Matthäus aus lauter Fotorahmen an. Aber vor allem lacht Bodo, der seinen Blick stets konzentriert auf die Eingangstür geheftet hat. Kaum spaziert ein Star herein, stürzt Bodo auf ihn zu, um ihn in sein Reich der tausend Sünden zu entführen. Da darf der Gast dann alles probieren, was süß und klebrig ist: Krapfen, Apfelstrudel mit Vanillesauce, Crêpes oder Waffeln, während ihm bauchfreie Brasilianerinnen Champagner aus Bodos Sektbar servieren.

This rather outlandish bakery between the Ochsenbraterei (roasted-ox stall), and the Augustiner beer tent in street # 2 is an Oktoberfest classic, decorated with cupids sitting on fluffy white clouds that hang from the ceiling. Whenever you need the 'loo' you will find many celebrities' faces grinning at you from their framed photographs. And Bodo himself is always in a good mood, his gaze constantly monitoring the entrance. As soon as celebrities cross the threshold Bodo welcomes them in and leads them into his realm of a thousand sins. His guests can then try anything that is sweet and sticky: doughnuts, 'apfelstrudel' with custard, crêpes or waffles while Brazilian girls with bare midriffs serve champagne from Bodo's bar.

Bratwurst Glöckl

Festwirt: Michael Beck
Reservierungsbüro:
T: 089-2 91 94 50, F: 089-2 90 47 36
Zeltbüro:
T: 089-50 22 22 88
Sitzplätze: 209
www.bratwurst-gloeckl.de

Es ist schwer, gleichgültig am Bratwurst Glöckl auf der Wirtsbudenstraße neben dem Winzerer Fähndl und dem Schottenhamel vorbeizugehen. Der Duft der Schweinsbratwürste, die dort über offenem Buchenholzfeuer brutzeln, kitzelt einfach zu verführerisch in der Nase. Die Zillertaler Gipfelstürmer zupfen auch zu gut ihre bayerischen Lieder. Und die Holzbänke knarren so urgemütlich, dass man einfach Platz nehmen muss. Wirt Michi Beck, ein Münchner Unikum, betreibt auch das Bratwurst Glöckl in der Innenstadt, dem das Wiesn-Glöckl nachempfunden wurde. Und die Speisekarte mit bayerischen Schmankerln ist hier wie dort deftig und gut.

Proprietor: Michael Beck
Reservations: (country code ++49)
T: (0)89-2 91 94 50, F: (0)89-2 90 47 36
Tent office: (country code ++49)
T: (0)89-50 22 22 88
Seating capacity: 209
www.bratwurst-gloeckl.de

It is not that easy, to walk past Bratwurst Glöckl on the Wirtsbudenstraße (food stall lange) between Winzerer Fähndl and the Schottenhamel tent. The smell from pork sausages being grilled over an open beechwood fire, creates an overwhelming temptation. The band 'Die Zillertaler Gipfelstürmer' plays Bavarian music. The wooden benches creak in such a homely way that you simply have to take a seat. The manager Michi Beck, a Munich original, also runs the Bratwurst Glöckl in the city centre. This was the model for the Oktoberfest-Glöckl. It offers the same wonderful Bavarian delicacies.

Hühner- und Entenbraterei AMMER

Festwirte: Sepp Schmidbauer
Reservierungsbüro:
T: 089-8 12 74 01, F: 089-8 13 22 26
Zeltbüro:
T: 089-50 07 72 92
Sitzplätze: 900
www.ammer-wiesn.de

Proprietor: Sepp Schmidbauer
Reservations: (country code ++49)
T: (0)89- 8 12 74 01, F: (0)89- 8 13 22 26
Tent office: (country code ++49)
T: (0)89-50 07 72 92
Seating capacity: 900
www.ammer-wiesn.de

Gibt es seit 1880 und ist damit eines der ältesten Zelte der Wiesn. Angefangen hat der Wirt als Geflügelhändler am Viktualienmarkt. Später eröffnete er die erste Hühnerbraterei der Welt. Die ist heute in der fünften Generation zum Traditions-Zelt auf der Wiesn geworden, in dem Augustiner-Bier im Holzfass ausgeschenkt wird und die Band Blue Moon für immer gute Laune sorgt. Wer nicht im süßen Bratduft auf der Wirtsbudenstraße zwischen Augustiner-Festhalle und Ochsenbraterei sitzen möchte, der kann sich auch das Hendl mit nach Hause nehmen und zum Bier aus der Dose daheim vor dem Fernseher seine ganz private Wiesn genießen.

This roast duck and chicken grill has been in business since 1880 and is therefore one of the oldest tents of the Oktoberfest. The original owner began as a poultry dealer at Munich's main food market, the Viktualienmarkt. Later on he opened the world's first chicken grill. His descendants in the fifth generation own one of the tents with the longest tradition on the 'Wiesn' and in which Augustiner beer is served from wooden barrels and the band 'Blue Moon' guarantees a good atmosphere. Those who prefer not to sit on the street with the eateries with all its sweet smells from the grills, between the Augustiner tent and the Ochsenbraterei, can take grilled chicken home and enjoy a really private Oktoberfest with canned beer in front of the TV.

Das Bayerische Gold

Es läuft frisch und kühl aus 605 Zapfhähnen: unser bestes Münchner Bier. Aber woher kommt der goldene Gerstensaft, aus Hopfen, Wasser, Malz und Hefe überhaupt?
Angefangen hat alles, so munkelt man, als vor vielen Tausenden von Jahren ein Mensch in einen sauren Brotteig spuckte. Aus Versehen wohlgemerkt. Es kam zur Gärung. Plötzlich war der Brotteig flüssig, man konnte den Brei trinken. Und er schmeckte sogar!
Schon die alten Ägypter genossen das Ur-Gebräu als alkoholische Erfrischung. Die Kelten und Germanen entdeckten im 3. Jahrhundert vor Christus Honig als Würze für ihren beliebten „Met". Für die Griechen war der Gerstensud Medizin gegen Fieber und Schlaflosigkeit und in Europa das Brauen von Bier Sache der Frauen. Die luden sogar zu richtigen „Bier-Kränzchen", wenn ihr Biersud gelungen war, um ihn gemeinsam zu probieren. Was nicht ganz ungefährlich war.
Erst sehr viel später hat man nämlich festgestellt, dass man Bier auch haltbar machen muss – und kann. 1487 wurde in München schließlich das erste Reinheitsgebot kodifiziert, erlassen von Herzog Albrecht IV., das 1516 sein Sohn Wilhelm IV. als bayerisches Reinheitsgebot übernahm.
Vor allem die Klöster erreichten eine hohe Kunst in der Wissenschaft des Brauens. Wegen seiner nahrhaften Eigenschaften war das Bier ein willkommenes Ersatznahrungsmittel der Mönche in der Fastenzeit, frei nach dem Motto „liquida non frangunt ienum" – Flüssiges bricht das Fasten nicht.
Benediktiner Mönche gründeten die erste Kloster-Brauerei im bayerischen Freising. 1328 folgten ihnen die Augustiner Mönche mit ihrem berühmten Augustiner-Bier. Noch heute ist ihr sogenanntes Starkbier sehr beliebt.

Bavarian Gold

It flows fresh and cool from 605 taps: Our finest Munich beer. Yet, where does this golden barley juice of hops, water, malt and yeast come from in the first place? It all began, or so they say, many thousands of years ago as somebody spat into a mixture of sour dough. Not on purpose, mind. The dough began to ferment. Suddenly it turned liquid and it was possible to drink the strange brew. It even tasted good!
In ancient Egypt people already enjoyed this primordial brew as alcoholic refreshment. The Celtic and Germanic tribes discovered in the third century BC that honey could be used to season their beloved mead. For the Greeks the barley extract served as medicine against fever and insomnia. In Europe women were in charge of beer. If the brewing was successful, they even invited each other to a kind of beer tasting to test their 'broth' together. But this was not quite free of danger.
Only very much later did people find out that beer can go off and that they had to–and indeed could–preserve it. At last, in 1487, the first ever 'Reinheitsgebot' (purity law) was codified in Munich, passed by Duke Albrecht IV, and which in 1516 was adopted by his son Wilhelm IV as Bavarian law.
It was mainly in the monasteries that a high standard of brewing was achieved. Due to its nutritional qualities, beer was a welcome supplement for the monks in the periods of fasting, and was in line with their maxim 'liquida non fragunt ienum', 'liquid does not break fasting'.
Benedictine monks founded the first monastic brewery in Freising, near Munich. In 1328 the Augustinian friars followed with their famous 'Augustiner' beer. Even today their so-called 'Starkbier' (ale- or stout-like beer) is very popular.

Bayerns Bier-Jahreszeiten:
Immer in der Fastenzeit im **März** zwischen Fasching und Ostern, wird auf dem Münchner Starkbierfest am Nockherberg das Starkbier mit der Endung -ator, z.B. das Salvator, Triumphator, Maximator, ausgeschenkt. Der Maibock bringt die Münchner gut durch den Wonnemonat **Mai**.
In der **Sommerzeit** bevorzugt der Münchner ein kühles Helles (zwischen 11 und 12,5 Stammwürze) oder ein frisch gezapftes Weißbier unter den Kastanien seines Biergartens.
Gegen Ende des Sommers beginnt dann Bayerns schönste Jahreszeit, die **Oktoberfest-Zeit**. Dort genießt der Bayer sein süffiges Oktoberfestbier, mit mindestens 13,5 Stammwürze. Nach einer kleinen Zwangspause wird dann in der Weihnachtszeit im **Dezember** das Festbier ausgeschenkt, das einen malzaromatischen Charakter hat.

Bavaria's beer seasons:
Every year, in the fasting period of **March**, between carnival and Easter, extra-strong beer is served at the 'Starkbier' festival on the Nockherberg in Munich. This type of beer is usually given names ending in '-ator' such as Salvator, Triumphator, Maximator. Elsewhere they may have the suffix '-bock' when for example the 'Maibock' brings the Munich citizens happily through the month of **May**.
In the **summertime** the Munich citizen prefers a cool lager (between 11 and 12.5 original wort) or a freshly drawn 'Weissbier' (wheat beer) under the chestnut trees of Munich's famous beer gardens.
Bavaria's most wonderful season begins towards the end of summer, the **Oktoberfest**. Here Bavarians enjoy the delightfully tasty 'Oktoberfestbier' (at least 13.5 original wort). After a short compulsory break in **December** at Christmas time 'Festbier' (festive beer), a beer with a somewhat malty-aromatic character, is served.

Bräurosl

Die Karussells

The Merry-Go-Rounds

Die Karussells

Was das Skifahren vorm Einkehren in die Hütte, ist auf dem Oktoberfest das Karussell-Fahren bevor man sich dann bis zum St. Nimmerleinstag in eines der Bierzelte pflanzt. Wir sind schließlich in Bayern und da ist man sportlich. Nur, Bierkrüge allein stemmen reicht nicht. Es gehört auch das Gefühl dazu, mit wehenden Schürzenbändern oder nackten Wadeln in einer der wackeligen Gondeln zu zittern. Die eine Faust am eiskalten Geländer, die andere verkrampft an der Taschenöffnung, damit beim Looping nicht Geld, Schlüssel und all die frisch ergatterten Telefonnummern herausfliegen. Aber es gibt auch gemütlichere Karussels wie die Krinoline. Sowie reichlich Auswahl für die Hau-den-Lukas-Extra-Starken, z. B. das Teufelsrad. **Drei Touren für jede Nervenklasse:**

The Merry-Go-Rounds

Just as skiing precedes the après-ski, taking a ride on one of the merry-go-rounds is what you do before you settle down in one of the beer tents not to get up again in a hurry. After all we are in Bavaria where people do exercise. Lifting beer mugs alone, however, is not enough. You also need the feeling of trembling in one of the wobbly cars with bare legs or dress ribbons fluttering in the wind. One hand clutching the ice-cold safety handlebar, the other tightly holding on to the pockets to keep money, keys and all the highly-prized new phone numbers from falling out during the next loop. There are, however, some less extreme, more sedate round-abouts: Small, nostalgic rides such as the Krinoline and a large selection for the Test-Your-Strength guys, e.g. the 'Teufelsrad'. **Here are three tours for each anxiety level:**

SKATER
PAULANER
MÜNCHEN
PAULANER
PAULANER

Für die Extrastarken oder die, die sich dafür halten:

Beginnen Sie doch gleich am **Powertower 2**. Das ist dieser Turm, der 66 Meter in die Höhe schnellt, um dann gleich wieder 63 Meter herunter zu fallen. Es reicht dennoch für einen Superblick über die Wiesn und ein wahnsinniges Bauchkribbeln auf dem Rückweg, das Gefühl „Freier Fall".

Im **Euro-Star** sitzt man wie Pinocchio: mit baumelnden Beinchen – und genauso ahnungslos. Plötzlich geht's nur noch Achterbahn! Und der Beste (für Mutige), also der schrecklichste (für Angsthasen) Platz, ist natürlich der ganz vorne, nur die Tiefe vor sich.

Cyberspace klingt harmlos, ist es aber nicht. Dahinter verbirgt sich ein Riesenpendel, das zu beiden Seiten ausschlägt, immer höher, immer höher. Bis es sich – überschlägt.

Und weil Sie es ja hart wollten, empfiehlt sich anschließend der **Polyp**. Er ist der gemeine Bruder der Krake, denn beim Polyp dreht sich alles um alles.

Das **Teufelsrad** gehört zu einem der ältesten Karussells. Es erfreute schon Karl Valentin: Freiwillige können dort solange auf einem rotierenden Rad fahren, bis sie die Fliehkraft, ein schwingender Schaumstoffball oder der Teufel mit einem Seil hinunter fegt. Große Geschicklichkeit ist gefordert.

Wer versagt, den lachen die Zuschauer aus. Was auch ziemlich grausam sein kann.

Ein unbedingtes Muss ist ein Besuch beim **Schichtl**. Da gibt es Dinge, die es eigentlich gar nicht gibt und von denen jeder weiß, dass es sie nicht gibt. Wie die Frau ohne Unterleib!

Wer dann noch immer nicht genug hat und sich so richtig die Magensäfte pürieren lassen will, der sollte sich noch ein paar Runden im **Breakdance** gönnen.

For the extra-tough or those who think they are

You should start straight away with **Power Tower II**. That is the tower that lifts you up into the air, 217 feet to the top, and instantly plummets 207 feet back down again. There is a brief moment for a great view over the Oktoberfest and an incredible feeling in the pit of your stomach on the way back down ... the free fall.

In the **Euro Star** roller coaster you sit in the car like Pinocchio: with dangling legs–and equally unsuspecting. Suddenly you are on a roller coaster! By the way the best place (for the brave) and therefore the most terrifying (for the faint-hearted) is of course right at the front, looking into the abyss.

Cyber Space sounds harmless but it is not. Its dark secret is a giant pendulum, swinging to the right and to the left, higher and higher, until it goes ... around overhead.

And as this is still for the tough the next thing to try is the **Polyp**. It is the mean version of the 'Krake'. Everything is spinning around, the cars on themselves and around each other.

The **Teufelsrad** is one of the Oktoberfest's oldest attractions. Even Karl Valentin, the famous comedian from the first half of the Twentieth Century, enjoyed the ride: It is really that old. Volunteers sit on a rotating disc for as long as possible until either centrifugal force, a swinging foam rubber ball or the devil with a lasso sweeps them off. Dexterity is essential.

Whoever falls off is mocked by the audience. It can be quite cruel.

An absolute must is a visit to **Schichtl**, a vaudeville show. Here you will see things that just cannot be and which everyone knows do not exist: Such as the woman without an abdomen.

If you still have not had enough and still want to make your stomach turn, then you should enjoy a few rides on the **Breakdance.**

Für Romantiker, Angsthasen oder große Kinder

Die **Krinoline** hat ihren Namen nach dem Reifrock der Frauen in der Biedermeierzeit, dessen Saum beim Tanz ähnliche Bewegungen machte: Sie ist eine Scheibe, die sich nach allen Seiten bewegt, wippt und dreht. So wird man auf ihr in plüschigen Sesseln hin und hergeschaukelt wie ein Baby in der Wiege. Dazu gibt's Blaskapellenmusik.
In der **Wilden Maus**, auf die auch Münchens Oberbürgermeister steht, sitzt man zwar wie auf einem Haken schlagenden Hasen. Der läuft aber keine Loopings, sondern „nur" Achterbahn.
Für die **Schiffsschaukel** gilt das Gleiche wie für eine gute Beziehung: Drei sind zu viel, einer zu wenig. Im Duett ist es perfekt: Sie darf sitzen, er kämpft sich ab. Ja, das gibt es noch.
Auch wenn die Gummispinnen und quietschenden Frankensteinköpfe langsam albern werden, es gibt kaum etwas Schöneres, als sich in der dunklen **Geisterbahn** Händchen haltend zu gruseln, oder?
Autoscooter fahren ist immer noch cool, weil man sich wie 17 und auf der ersten Klassenreise fühlt. Mädchen gegen Jungs – das macht immer Spaß.
Im großen **Riesenrad** kann man 50 Meter über München träumen und nachts funkelt unter einem das bunte Oktoberfest.
Rosenschießen, liebe Herren, ist ein alter Brauch. Die Wiesn-Statistik allerdings belegt: Frauen treffen besser.
Wer schließlich die Zeit, weil sie so schön ist, noch mal anhalten möchte, für den ist das **Star World** die richtige Achterbahn: ohne Looping, ohne Tiefen. Man saust in einem geschlossenen Raum wie zeit- und schwerelos durchs Weltall.

For the romantic, the easily frightened or the big kids

The **Krinoline** has its name from the women's early Victorian skirt, whose hem would move in a similar way in a dance: The ride is a disc moving in all directions, twisting and turning. Here you will be swung to and fro in plush seating, like a baby in a cradle–accompanied by brass band music.
Riding on the **Wilde Maus**, which by the way Munich's mayor is fond of, is rather like a fleeing rabbit, doubling all the time. Luckily however, it does not go round in a loop; it is 'only' a roller coaster.
For the **Schiffsschaukel** (swing boat) the same is true as for a good relationship: Three is a crowd and one is not enough. A couple is perfect: She takes a seat–he tires himself out. Yes, you can still get that.
Even when rubber spiders and squawking Frankenstein heads really are a bit silly there is nevertheless nothing better than to be in the dark **Geisterbahn** (ghost train), holding hands and being scared together, now is there ...
Here they are called **Autoscooters**, but driving in the bumper cars is still rather cool, since you feel like you are 17 again and on your first school trip: Boys against girls–that is always a lot of fun.
In the **Riesenrad**, the big Ferris wheel, you can dream at 164 feet above Munich. At night the many coloured lights of the Oktoberfest sparkle beneath you.
Gentlemen, go to win a rose, **Rosenschießen**, at the shooting gallery. It is an old tradition. Oktoberfest statistics prove, however, that women are far better at it.
Finally, if you are having a good time and do not want it to stop then **Star World** is just the roller coaster for you: no loops, no plummeting. You dash around in an enclosed space, like flying time- and weightlessly through the universe.

Für die Oldies, die Handschuhkarussellfahrer, aber vor allem für die Kleinen

Direkt neben dem Fünfer-Looping steht das kleine **Russische Riesenrad** mit seinen hübschen bunten Gondeln und der alten Noten-Konzertorgel. Als das knapp 14 Meter hohe Rad 1926 erstmals auf der Wiesn stand, galt es als größtes Riesenrad Deutschlands.
Im kleinen **Kettenkarussell** können fürsorgliche Eltern neben ihren Kindern fliegen – die trotzdem quäken, weil sie doch ins Große wollten.
Auf der **Münchner Rutsche** wird man 23 Meter wie auf einem Fließband hochgezogen und rutscht auf Filzdecken wieder runter.
Immer wieder beliebt ist das **Ponyreiten**: an der Bavaria können die Kleinen auf Isländern und Haflingern ihre Runde drehen ...
... oder in der **Märcheneisenbahn** so lang im Kreis fahren, bis die sieben Zwerge Purzelbäume drehen.
Im Irrgarten des **Spiegelkabinetts** kann man die Menschen lachen hören, als kitzelte man sie unter den Füßen. Dabei stehen sie nur vor verzehrten Spiegeln und ziehen lange Nasen.
Außerdem gibt es täglich **Kasperltheater** auf dem Oktoberfest, drei **Kinderspielplätze** sowie **Führungen** für die Kleinen, die mal hinter die Kulissen blicken wollen (Anmeldungen unter T: 089-2 32 39 00).

Übrigens, immer dienstags, am sogenannten Familientag, gibt es zwischen 12 und 18 Uhr auf der ganzen Wiesn ermäßigte Preise an allen Fahrgeschäften, Zelten und Imbissstellen.

For the slightly-advanced-in-years, the not-so-sure-of-it-all, but most of all for the children

Directly next to the five-loop roller coaster there is the little **Russische Riesenrad** (Russian Ferris wheel) with its pretty, coloured cars and its old concert organ. In 1926, when it appeared at the Oktoberfest for the first time, it was with its almost 46 foot high wheel the biggest Ferris wheel in Germany.
On the smaller **Kettenkarussell** (chairoplane) concerned parents can ride alongside their children–who squeal nonetheless as what they really want is to ride on the bigger one.
At the **Münchner Rutsche** for 75 feet you are pulled forwards and upwards like on a conveyor belt and you slide back down on felt mats.
A much-loved attraction is **Pony riding**: at the Bavaria statue the little ones can ride on Iceland ponies and Haflinger horses ...
... or on the **Märcheneisenbahn** (fairy tale railway) they can ride around in circles until the seven dwarves turn somersaults.
In the illusion of the **Spiegelkabinett** (house of mirrors) you can hear people laughing as if their feet were being tickled; though they simply stand grimacing in front of distorting mirrors.
Further attractions at the Oktoberfest include **Kasperltheater** ('Punch and Judy' show), three **children's playgrounds**, as well as **guided tours** for kids who want to take a look behind the scenes (for reservations call: (++49) (0) 89-2 32 39 00).

By the way: on Tuesdays, the so-called family days, between 12:00 and 18:00, reduced prices all over the Oktoberfest and at all the side shows, rides, tents and food stalls.

Die Wiesn für Zugroaste

The Oktoberfest for 'Outsiders'

Der Wiesn-Knigge

Das Oktoberfest ist das schönste Fest der Welt. Auch wenn es ein bisschen chaotisch ist. Für den unerfahrenen Besucher scheint es hier nur eine Regel zu geben: dass es keine Regel gibt. Aber das wirkt nur so. Die Wiesn hat ihre eigenen Gesetze und ihren Knigge. Und der geht so:

The Oktoberfest book of good manners

The Oktoberfest is the world's greatest festival and, even if it can be quite chaotic, for the inexperienced visitors it appears to have only one rule: There are no rules. It only seems that way however. The Oktoberfest has its own set of rules and its own code of conduct. Here are the Dos and Don'ts:

Dos

Tanz, Baby!

Aber ja, auf der Wiesn darf getanzt werden. Allerdings bitte nur auf den Bänken. Auf den Tischen ist es erstens streng verboten. Und zweitens gefährlich, wenn nach der dritten, vierten, fünften Maß der Gleichgewichtssinn nicht mehr jeden Kampf gegen die Schwerkraft gewinnen kann.

Dance, Baby!

Of course you can dance at the Oktoberfest. You can even get up onto the benches, but dancing on the tables is strictly prohibited. Furthermore it is dangerous, when after the third, fourth, fifth litre of beer, one's balance no longer wins each struggle against gravity.

Immer mit der Masse

Um über das Oktoberfest zu gehen, sollten Sie sich mit der Masse bewegen: Lassen Sie sich vom Strom der Menschen mitschieben. So kommen Sie am schnellsten voran. Außer es gelingt Ihnen, sich in den Windschatten laufender Sanitäter zu hängen, die gerade eine Bierleiche durch die Menge reichen.

Always go with the flow

In order to get around at the Oktoberfest, you should move with the crowd: Let yourself drift along in the flow of visitors. This is the best way to move around, unless you manage to get into the slipstream of a group of paramedics carrying one of the beer casualties away on a stretcher.

Vergessen Sie Ihre guten Manieren

Eine Maß wird g'suffa, ein Hendl mit den Fingern gerissen. Aber wem das zu barbarisch ist, der darf auch Besteck benutzen, das gibt es sogar aus Metall. Und keine Angst: Die Maß aus Plastik, wie auf dem Moskauer Oktoberfest, wird's nie geben. Auch wenn der Krug 1 Kilo wiegt: Geprostet wird seit 1892 mit Glas.

Forget your manners

The mug of beer is knocked back and the roast chicken is torn apart with the fingers. However, if this is too barbaric for you, you can always ask for knife and fork. The cutlery is made of metal. There is no need to worry about plastic beer mugs, as at the Moscow Oktoberfest, you will never find them here, even if the mugs themselves weigh over two pounds: Here people have been toasting each other with glass since 1892.

Diridari im Dirndl

Eins vorweg: Das Oktoberfest ist kein Ort für Gleichstellungsbeauftragte. Somit müssen Frauen für Toilettenbesuche zahlen, Männer dürfen umsonst. Frauen sollten darum stets Kleingeld, das sogenannte Diridari, in der Dirndltasche parat haben, für die Klofrau. Dafür haben die Männer ja die Maß gezahlt, oder?

'Diridari' in the 'dirndl'

First of all, the 'Wiesn' is no place to fight for the equality of women: Women must pay for their visit to the toilets, men don't. Women should therefore always have some small change (the 'Diridari') in their 'dirndl' pocket, for the attendant. That is why the men pay for the beer, isn't it?

Halligalli auf dem Häusl

Vor allem Männer lieben die Wiesn. Nicht nur, weil man da so nett im Kollektiv Flüssiges zu sich nehmen, sondern auch Flüssiges abgeben kann: Büx an Büx vor der Rinne in Reihe. Wundern Sie sich nicht, wenn Sie dabei verrückte Bekanntschaften machen. Das ist normal. Und Wildpinkeln übrigens sehr teuer!

Messing about in the outhouse

Men particularly like the Oktoberfest. Not only because it is so nice to collectively absorb fluids, but relinquishing them is something like teamwork as well: Side by side in neat rows, in front of the urinal. And do not be surprised if you meet one or two crazy guys. That is quite normal. By the way urinating anywhere else can become expensive!

Feiern, aber bitte mit Würde!

Heißt für die Damen auch: Vorsicht mit zu viel Make-up wegen Hitze und Alkohol! Besser mehr – man muss es mal sagen – Deo und Pfefferminzbonbons einsetzen. Für alle gilt: Auch mal Wasser trinken oder an die frische Luft – das schützt vor Gesichtsentgleisung. Und, liebe Männer, sachte mit der Nachbarin. Nach dem Rausch kommt nur die Reue!

Celebrate, but please with decorum

This also means for the ladies: Go easy on the make-up, too much heat and alcohol! It would be better–it must be said, I'm afraid–for people to use more deodorant and mints. It is important for everyone to drink water occasionally and to get some fresh air. This should help prevent binge drinking. Gentlemen, go easy on the girl sitting next to you. You will only regret it once the intoxication is over!

Süße Sünde

Was sind Kalorien? Gönnen Sie sich gebrannte Mandeln, Zuckerwatte, Liebesäpfel. Denn so, mit dem Schatz an der Hand und etwas klebrig Süßem im Mund schlendert es sich am schönsten über die Wiesn. Wenn er dann noch eine rote Rose schießt und ihr ein „I mog di"-Herz um den Hals hängt, fährt die Seele Looping.

Sweet indulgences

What are calories anyway? Just enjoy caramelised roast almonds, candy floss and candy apples. Holding hands with your sweetheart and with something sweet and sticky in your mouth is simply the best way to stroll around the Oktoberfest. And when he wins a rose for her and he puts an 'I mog di' (I love you) gingerbread heart around her neck the soul dances.

Plätze besetzt halten

Die Wiesn ist nicht der Ballermann, denn München ist nicht Mallorca. Hier wird darum auch kein Bier mit dem Strohhalm gezuzelt, noch sich der Platz an der Sonne mit dem Badetuch ergeizt. Bierbänke sind keine Sonnenliegen und darum frei. Die Okkupation durch Mäntel, Taschen oder Bierkrüge ist nur eins: spießig!

Keeping your seats reserved

The Oktoberfest is not an all-inclusive holiday and Munich is not Majorca. Beer should not be slurped through a straw and neither should a place in the sun be 'occupied' with a towel. Beer benches are not deck chairs and should be kept free. Reserving seats with coats, bags or beer mugs is just that: Narrow minded!

Haupteingänge

Vergessen Sie, dass Zelte Haupteingänge haben. Dort hängt als erstes das Schild: „Wegen Überfüllung geschlossen". Benutzen Sie die Seiteneingänge oder noch besser: Kommen Sie wie die echten Münchner mittags auf die Wiesn. Denn dann ist sie noch so friedlich-harmonisch wie sie früher immer war.

Main entrances to the beer tents

Just forget that beer tents have main entrances. In any case, the first thing you will find there is a sign saying 'wegen Überfüllung geschlossen' (temporarily closed due to overcrowding). Use the side entrances or better still: Arrive at lunchtime like the Munich natives. At this time of day the 'Wiesn' is so peaceful and quiet as it once used to be.

Nasehochs!

Sie gehen auf die Wiesn. Auf ein Volksfest – das kommt von: Volks-nä-he! Sich rausputzen oder „aufbrezn" ist okay. Aber die Nase hoch tragen geht gar nicht. Besser sie fällt ins nächste Dekollete. Auf der Wiesn sind schließlich die schönsten Madeln. Das Fest ist zum Anbandeln da.

Looking down their noses

They go to the Oktoberfest, a 'volksfest'–which means that they get close to the people. Dressing up is alright, but looking down your nose is not the done thing. Your nose should only inspect the cleavage sitting next to you. After all, the prettiest girls can be found at the Oktoberfest, which is made for flirting.

Tapsen Sie nicht in die Souvenirfalle

Sepplhüte, blinkende Teufels-Hörner, „Do-legst-di-nieda"-Jodel-Löwen, rülpsende Plüschmaßkrüge und sonstiger Schmarrn an Oktoberfest-Andenken sind ja ganz lustig. Aber man muss sich bitte nicht zur Schießbudenfigur hochstilisieren. Das Oktoberfest ist kein Karneval.

Do not fall into the souvenir trap

Floppy hats, flashing devil's horns, 'I-don't-believe-this'-yodelling lions, burping fluffy beer mugs and other such Oktoberfest souvenir nonsense can be quite funny, but it is unnecessary to adorn yourself with so many that it looks like you were selling them. The 'Wiesn' is not a carnival.

Kein Witz: Vermeiden Sie die Wies-e-n!

Auch wenn der Name anderes vermuten lässt: Die „Wies-n“ findet nicht auf einer Wies-e statt. Das Festgelände ist asphaltiert. Und die paar Flecken am Rand, auf denen tatsächlich noch Gras wächst, sind zwingend zu meiden. Außer Sie möchten erleben, wie Menschen aussehen, die drei Maß zu lang im Bierzelt waren.

No joke: Avoid the 'Wiesn'!

Even when the name suggests otherwise: The Oktoberfest, known locally as the 'Wiesn' (meadow) does not actually take place on a meadow. The festival area was asphalted over long ago. And those few small bits at the edge where grass still does grow are to be avoided at all costs—unless you really want to see what Oktoberfest visitors look like when they had three litres too many.

Don't drink and drive!

Riskieren Sie nicht Ihren Führerschein! U-Bahn fahren zur Wiesn-Zeit ist außerdem ein Erlebnis, wenn der Zugführer übers Mikro seine Faxen macht. Wiesn-Profis bestellen sich ein Taxi für den späten Rückweg vor (Nummer merken!). Denn nach dem letzten Wiesn-Lied wollen ALLE lieber heim taxeln statt heim torkeln.

Do not drink and drive

Do not risk your driving licence! Taking the underground to the Oktoberfest is an experience in itself. The driver tells jokes over the speaker. 'Wiesn' experts order their taxi for the trip back home in advance (make a note of the number) because everyone wants to be driven home rather then straggle home after the last beer tent song ends.

Für Grabscher gibt's a Watschen

Auf der Wiesn ist es ein bisschen wie in der freien Wildbahn. Da wird gebalzt, angebandelt und gegraben. Was nicht gut ankommt: unkoordiniertes Grapschen. Heißt: Das Berühren der Figüren mit den Pfoten ist verboten! Und der Strafkatalog geht so:
Erst gibt's 'ne Mahnung.
Dann gibt's a Watschen.

The molester gets slapped

The Oktoberfest can be one great adventure. Advances and approaches are made. People flirt and chat each other up. What is not acceptable, however, is unwelcome fondling. Therefore: Do not touch—keep your hands off! The punishment: first a verbal warning then a slap in the face.

Eigenes Essen mitbringen

Verwechseln Sie die Wiesn auch nicht mit einem Biergarten oder Ausflug in einen Tier-Nationalpark. Gegessen wird, was rotbäckige, strammwadige Kellnerinnen auf Riesentabletts vorbeijonglieren. Sie sind die wahren Helden der Wiesn. Und mit gutem Trinkgeld kommt richtig Dampf unter ihre Sohlen.

Bringing your own food

Do not confuse the Oktoberfest with a beer garden or a trip to a nature reserve. You eat what red-cheeked, strong-legged waitresses serve, who juggle the food on giant trays above your heads. They are the real heroines of the 'Wiesn'. And a good tip will put a fresh surge of energy into their step.

Das kleine Bierzelt-Lexikon

Damit Sie im Bierzelt nicht nur mittrinken, sondern auch bestellen, anstoßen, reden, und flirten können.

Boarisch für Zugroaste – Bayerisch für Nicht-Münchner:

Bestellen:

Entschuldi'gens?! Entschuldigen sie bitte?
Oa Maß bitt'sche. Ein Bier, bitte.
Für mi a Radla! Für mich ein Radler!
Hamma auf der Wiesn ned! Gibt es auf dem Oktoberfest nicht!
I hätt gern a hoibs Hendl. Ich hätte gern ein halbes Hähnchen.
Für mi an Schweinsbratn mit Knödel. Für mich einen Schweinsbraten mit Kartoffelknödel.
Und oa Brezn! Und eine Brezn!
Und später oan Kaffee im Haferl und oa Auszogene! Später bitte eine große Tasse Kaffee mit einer süßen bayerischen Hefespezialität.
Gibt's hier a Schweinswürstl mit Kraut? Gibt es denn auch Bratwürstchen mit Sauerkraut?
Freilich! Ja klar.
Jetzt stoß' ma erst amoi o! Jetzt stoßen wir erst einmal an!
Prost! Prost!
Auf de Bänke! Auf die Bierbänke!

Mit der Blaskapelle:

Ein Prosit, ein Prosit der Gemütlichkeit. Ein Prosit, ein Prosit, der Gemütlichkeit!
Oans, zwoa, droa, g'suffa! Prost!

Unterhalten:

Hier is a riesen Gaudi. Hier ist die Stimmung toll.
Wo kimmst denn Du her? Woher kommst Du?
Aus Minga. Aus München.
Is do no a Platzerl frei? Ist hier noch ein Plätzchen frei?
Für di scho! Für Dich schon!
Hock di her, samma mehr! Setz Dich ruhig zu uns!
I mus bieseln! Ich muss mal austreten!
Host a Diridari? Hast Du auch Kleingeld dabei?

Flirten:

Spinn i, hat die Hoiz vor der Hüttn! Wahnsinn, hat das Mädchen viel Oberweite!
Mit dera möcht i obandln. Die will ich kennen lernen.
Sacradi, bist Du a feschs Derndl! Wahnsinn, Du bist eine tolle Frau!
Und Du a Pfundskerl! Und Du bist ein toller Typ!
A Busserl könnt jetzt a ned schadn! Ein Kuss wäre jetzt genau das Richtige!
I bin do ned narrisch! Ich bin doch nicht verrückt!
Schau'ma mal. Warten wir mal ab.
I mog Di! Ich finde Dich gut!
I mog di a! Ich finde Dich auch gut!
Schreib ma Dei Nummer auf'n Bierdeckl. Schreib mir Deine Telefonnummer auf den Bierdeckel.
Oder kimmst glei mit? Oder kommst Du gleich mit mir?
Jetzt gibt's aber glei oa Watschen! Jetzt bekommst Du aber gleich eine Ohrfeige!
Machs gut Spatzerl. Machs gut Schätzchen.
Pfiaddi Mausi. Servus, mein Hase.

The little dictionary for the beer tent

So that you not only can drink with the locals, but now you can also order drinks and food, toast, talk, and flirt.
Bavarian for foreigners – Boarisch für Zugroaste:

Ordering:

Excuse me, please! Entschuldi'gens?!
A beer please! Oa Mass bitt'sche.
A shandy for me! Für mi a radla!
Not on offer at the Oktoberfest! Hamma auf der Wiesn ned!
I'd like half a chicken, please. I hätt gern a hoibs hendl.
I'd like schweinsbraten (roast pork) with potato dumplings, please. Für mi an Schweinsbratn mit Knödel.
And a pretzel! Und a Brezn!
And to follow, a coffee with a doughnut, please. Und später a Kaffee im Haferl und a Auszogene!
Do you have pork sausages with sauerkraut? Gibt's hier a Schweinswürstl mit Kraut?
Yes, of course! Freilich!
So, let's raise our glasses first! Jetzt stoss ma erst amoi o!
Cheers! Prost!
Up, onto the benches! Auf de Bänke!

Choruses sung together with the band:

Cheers, cheers to our well-being. Ein Prosit, ein Prosit der Gemütlichkeit.
One, and two, and get it down!
Oans, zwoi, g'suffa!

Conversation:

Great atmosphere here. Hier is a riesen Gaudi.
Where do you come from? Wo kimmst denn Du her?
From Munich. Aus Minga.
Is this seat taken? Is do no a Platzerl frei?
Not for you, it isn't! Für di scho!
Come, sit down, the more, the merrier! Hock di her, samma mehr!
I have to go to the toilet! I mus bieseln!
Do you have money on you? Host a Diridari?

Flirting:

Wow, just look at this cleavage! Spinn i, hat die Hoiz vor der Hüttn!
I'd like to get to know her. Mit dera möcht i obandln.
Wow, you're really good-looking! Sacradi, bist Du a feschs Derndl!
And you're a great guy! Und Du a Pfundskerl!
A kiss would be just the thing now! A Busserl könnt jetzt a ned schadn!
I'm not crazy! I bin do ned narrisch!
We'll see. Schau'ma mal.
I like you! I mog Di!
I like you, too! I mog di a!
Write your phone number on this beer mat. Schreib ma Dei Nummer auf'n Bierdeckl.
Or do you want to come with me straight away? Oder kimmst glei mit?
Now, you're in for a slap! Jetzt gibt's aber glei a Watschen!
Take care, darling ... Machs gut Spatzerl ...
Bye, bye love. Pfiaddi Mausi.

Bavaria

Der Wiesn-Kalender

Wenn Sie glauben, Sie hätten nun schon alles gesehen, was unser Oktoberfest zu bieten hat, dann irren Sie. Es gibt weitaus mehr als nur Bierzelte und Karussells. Nämlich **viele schöne Veranstaltungen** rund um die Wiesn. Die wichtigsten Termine auf einen Blick:

Tag 1: Erster Wiesn-Samstag

10:45 – 11:45 Uhr

Einzug der Festwirte und Brauereien von der Josephspitalstraße über die östliche Sonnenstraße, sowie die Schwanthalerstraße auf die Wirtsbudenstraße der Theresienwiese.

12 Uhr

Eröffnung der Wiesn im Festzelt Schottenhamel. Anstich durch den Oberbürgermeister.

Day 1: First Saturday

10:45 – 11:45

Arrival of the beer tent managers and breweries starting in town at the Josephspitalstraße, via the eastern part of Sonnenstraße, then the Schwanthaler Straße into Wirtsbudenstraße (food stall lane) on the Theresienwiese (Oktoberfest park).

12:00

Official opening of the Oktoberfest in the Schottenhamel tent. Tapping of the first barrel by Munich's mayor.

Tag 2: Erster Wiesn-Sonntag

10 – 12 Uhr

Trachten- und Schützenumzug mit 8000 Mitwirkenden, sowie Bayerns Ministerpräsident Edmund Stoiber und Münchens Oberbürgermeister Christian Ude vom Siegestor/Ludwigstraße über die Schwanthalerstraße zum Esperantoplatz. Tribünen-Tickets über München Ticket, T: 089-54 81 81 81 oder www.muenchenticket.de

Day 2: First Sunday

10:00 – 12:00

Traditional dress and regional shooting clubs' parade with 8,000 participants including Bavaria's premier and Munich's mayor Christian Ude, starting from the Siegestor and Ludwigstraße via Schwanthaler Straße to Esperantoplatz. Grandstand tickets can be booked with München Ticket, T: (++49)(0)89-54 81 81 81 or www.muenchenticket.de

Tag 3: Erster Wiesn-Montag

12 – 15 Uhr

Bewirtung sozial bedürftiger Senioren in allen großen Festhallen auf Kosten des jeweiligen Wirtes.

Day 3: First Monday

12:00 – 15:00

Food and drink for senior citizens on benefits in all the large beer tents financed by the respective beer tent manager.

The Oktoberfest Calendar

If you think you have now seen everything our Oktoberfest has to offer, then you are wrong. There is a lot more than just beer tents and Ferris wheels. There are **a lot of great events** happening all around the Oktoberfest. Here are the most important dates at a glance:

Tag 4: Erster Wiesn-Dienstag

12 – 18 Uhr

Erster Familientag mit ermäßigten Fahr-, Eintritts- und Imbiss-Preisen.

Day 4: First Tuesday

12:00 – 18:00

First family day with reduced prices on food and all rides.

Tag 6: Erster Wiesn-Donnerstag

10 Uhr

Ökumenischer Oktoberfest- und Gedenkgottesdienst im Hippodrom für Schausteller und Wirte.

Day 6: First Thursday

10:00

Ecumenical Oktoberfest and remembrance church service in the Hippodrom for fairground personnel and tent managers.

Tag 9: Zweiter Wiesn-Sonntag

11 – 12 Uhr

Standkonzert der Wiesnkapellen zu Füßen der Bavaria.

Day 9: Second Sunday:

11:00 – 12:00

Bandstand concert of the 'Wiesn' bands below the Bavaria statue.

Tag 11: Zweiter Wiesn-Dienstag

12 – 18 Uhr

Zweiter Familientag mit ermäßigten Fahr-, Eintritts- und Imbisspreisen.

Day 11: Second Tuesday

12:00 – 18:00

Second family day with reduced prices on all food and rides.

Tag 16: Dritter Wiesn-Sonntag

12 Uhr

Böllerschießen auf den Stufen der Bavaria anlässlich des Oktoberfest-Landesschießens des Bayerischen Sportschützenbundes.

Day 16: Third Sunday

12:00

The firing of gun salutes on the steps of the Bavaria statue on the occasion of the Bavarian shooting sport association's Oktoberfest competition.

Karlstr.
Marsstr.
Deroystr.
Wredestr.
Arnulfstr.
Hopfenstr.
Seidlstr.
Elisenstr.
Dachauer Str.
Augustenstr.
Luisenstr.
Meiserstr.
Sophienstr.
N
Grasser Str.
Prielmayerstr.
Hauptbahnhof
Zollstr.
Bayerstr.
Westendstr.
Martin-Greif-Str.
Hermann-Lingg-Str.
Schlosserstr.
Sonnenstr.
Schwanthalerstr.
Schwan- thalerstr.
Parkstr.
Schießstättstr.
Land- wehrstr.
Gollierstr.
Bavariaring
St.-Pauls-Str.
Paul-Heyse-Str.
Goethestr.
Schillerstr.
Mathildenstr.
Alter Messe-platz
Petten- koferstr.
Heimeranstr.
Theresienwiese
Uhland-str.
Rückert-str.
Heinr.-Str.
Nußbaumstr.
Theresienhöhe
OKTOBERFEST
Beet- hovenstr.
Goethestr.
Flegen str.
Augsburgerstr.
Matthias-Pschorr-Str.
Esperanto-platz
Schubert-
Haydnstr.
Mozart- str.
Herzog-
Kobellstr.
Maistr.
Frauenlobstr.
Waltherstr.
Herm.-Schmid-Str.
Lindwurmstr.
Häberlstr.
Thalkirchner Str.
Hans-Klein-Str.
Radlkoferstr.
Fischer-Str.
Stieler-str.
Tumblingerstr.
Kapuzinerstr.
Bavariaring
Gülli-str.
Adlzreiterstr.
Zenettistr.
Maistr.
Pestalozzistr.
Pfeuferstr.
Berlepschstr.
Lipowskystr.
Poccistr.
Grimm-str.
Schmellerstr.
Tumblingerstr.
Geyerstr.
Bavariastr.
Ruppertstr.
Lindwurmstr.
Thalkirchner Str.
Isartalstr.

Map of Munich

Bars, Clubs

Shops

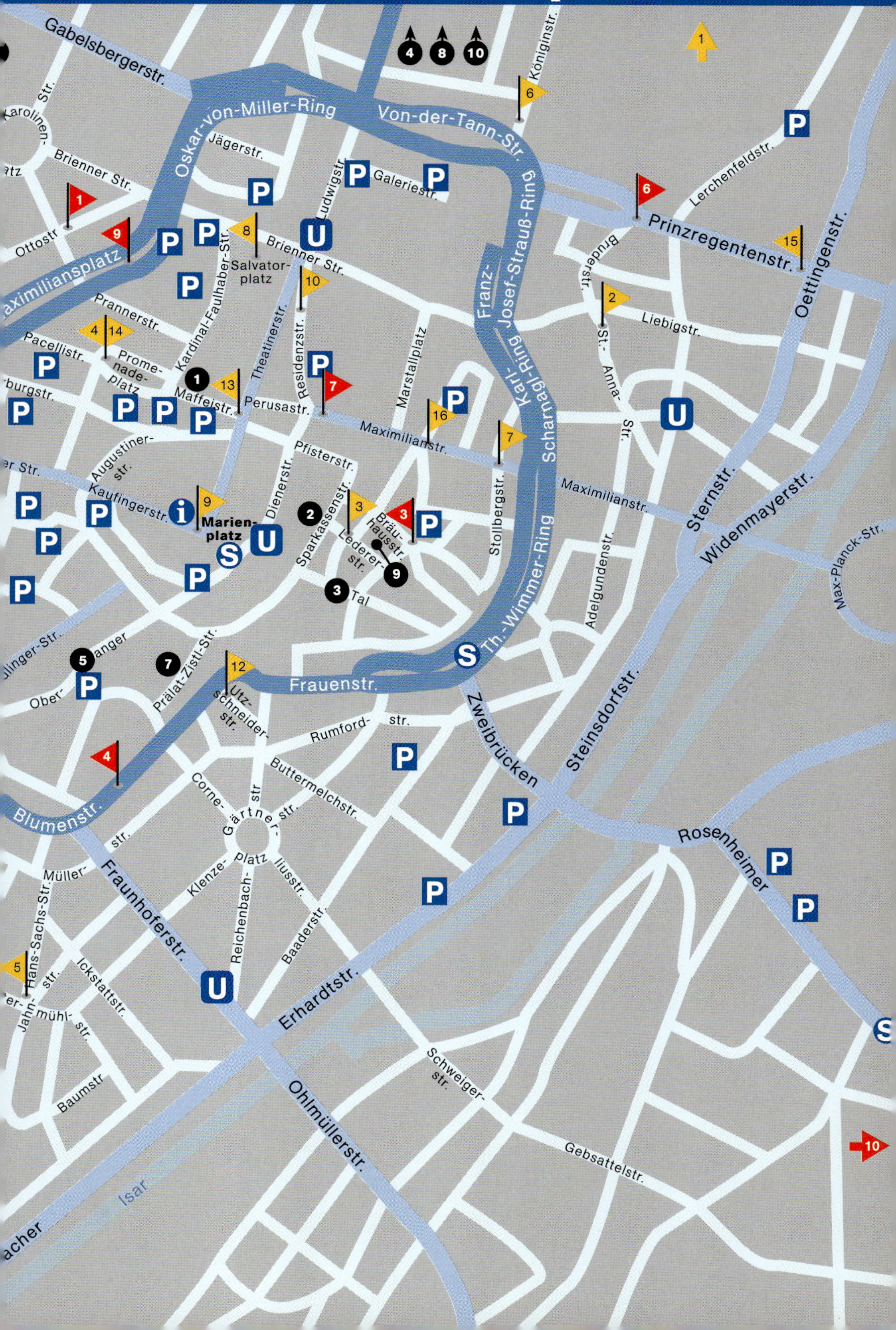

Insider-Treffs rund um die Wiesn:

Auch während der Wiesn gibt es, man will es nicht glauben, eine wiesnfreie Zeit, wenn auch das Wiesn-Fieber bleibt: Jeden Abend nämlich, wenn die Zelte schließen, bis sie am nächsten Morgen wieder öffnen. Wo Wiesn-Insider diese Stunden verbringen, um ausgelassen in Münchens Innenstadt weiter zu feiern, dann vielleicht auch mal ein paar Stündchen zu schlafen und sich schließlich für den nächsten Tag zu stärken, das verrate ich Ihnen jetzt:

Nach der Wiesn – hier geht die Party weiter:

Die Bars:

1 **Lenbach** ist der Geheimtipp für die besten After-Wiesn-Parties und der Kontrast schlechthin: cooles Ambiente statt rustikaler Zeltlook. Täglich ab 22 Uhr.
Ottostraße 6, T: 089-54 91 300

Lenbach

2 **Barysphär** ist ein Food-Club mit DJ-Bar im Kellergewölbe. Chic, lässig und nah zur Wiesn, weshalb sich hier viele Dirndl und Lederhosen nach dem Oktoberfest austoben.
Tumblingerstraße 36, T: 089-76 77 50 21

3 **Bar Harlander** ist wie eine Privatparty in einem proppevollen, pinkfarbenen Wohnzimmer. Klein und sehr angesagt, darum immer zu voll.
Bräuhausstraße 8, T: 089-23 24 16 52

Insider tips for venues around the Oktoberfest:

You would not believe it, but even during the Oktoberfest there is such a thing as a break from the 'Wiesn'. Although the festival fever itself continues every night, from the time the beer tents close to the next day when they open again for business. Below you will find all the places in Munich's centre where the Oktoberfest experts go to party through the night, to get a few hours sleep and eventually get ready for the next day:

After the Oktoberfest–here is where the party continues (country code ++49):

Bars:

1 **Lenbach** is an insider tip for the best after-Oktoberfest parties and a complete contrast: cool ambience instead of rustic-tent look–every day from 22:00.
Ottostraße 6, T: (0)89-54 91 300

2 **Barysphär** is a club-cum-restaurant with a DJ bar in the vaulted basement. Hip, cool and close to the Oktoberfest, that is why many revellers in 'dirndls' and 'lederhosen' come here after the Oktoberfest.
Tumblinger Straße 36, T: (0)89-76 77 50 21

3 **Bar Harlander** is like a private party in a pink-coloured lounge chock-a-block with people. Small and very hip, therefore always too packed.
Bräuhausstraße 8, T: (0)89-23 24 16 52

4 **Padres** is the experimental extension to the Oktoberfest. Here they dance to Marianne Rosenberg and Rex Gildo. Charming barmen lure you with dangerously colourful drinks.
Blumenstraße 43, T: (0)89-26 42 63

5 **Restaurant Lamms** The later the hour, the more bizarre and eccentric the

4 **Padres** ist die verbrüdernde Verlängerung nach der Wiesn. Hier wird zu Marianne Rosenberg und Rex Gildo weitergefeiert. Süße Barmänner locken mit gefährlich bunten Drinks.
Blumenstraße 43, T: 089-26 42 63

5 **Restaurant Lamms** Je später die Nacht desto skurriler das Publikum. Hier trifft sich der hungrige Hangover und die Nachtmahlgesellschaft in allen Variationen. Open 24 hours.
Sendlinger Torplatz 11, T: 089-58 19 63

Die Clubs:

6 **P1** ist Münchens Club No.1 mit Riesen-Partyterrasse, gemütlichen Flirtecken, zwei Diskotheken. Hier will alles rein. Aber wer wirklich reinkommt, das entscheiden Less und Dirk, die unbestechlichsten Türsteher Münchens. Dirndl und Lederhosen sind gern gesehen!
Prinzregentenstraße 1, T: 089-21 11 140

P1

7 **8 Seasons** Tanzen und feiern über den Dächern Münchens kann im alten Postamt, wer es schafft, an den Türstehern Nico, Alex oder Dana vorbeizukommen. Di und Do ist bis 4 Uhr, Fr und Sa sogar bis 6 Uhr geöffnet!
Maximilianstraße 2, T: 0176-23 23 23 23

8 **Mia** In ihrem neuen Club schenkt Model Giulia Siegel auf zwei Etagen mit Restaurant Münchens Ausgeh-Szene so richtig ein. Und ab 3 Uhr morgens gibt es frische Weißwürste! Vom Oktoberfest bequem zu Fuß erreichbar.
Herzogspitalstraße 6, T: 089-44 23 23 11

guests. The hungry hangover meets the night-cap community in all its many variations. Open 24 hours.
Sendlinger Torplatz 11, T: (0)89-58 19 63

Clubs:

6 **P1** is Munich's No.1 club with an enormous party terrace, cosy corners to flirt in and two discotheques. Everyone tries to get in here, but who really gets in? Less and Dirk decide, Munich's most unbribeable bouncers. 'Dirndls' and 'lederhosen' are very welcome!
Prinzregentenstraße 1, T: (0)89-21 11 140

7 **8 Seasons** Everyone who makes it past the bouncers Nico, Alex or Dana can dance and party above Munich's rooftops in the old post office building. Open Tuesdays and Thursdays until 04:00, Fridays and Saturdays until 06:00!
Maximilianstraße 2, T: (0)176-23 23 23 23

8 Seasons

8 **Mia** In her new club, two floors with restaurant, model Giulia Siegel really knows how to please Munich's party people. And from 03:00 in the morning fresh white veal sausages are available! Within walking distance from the Oktoberfest.
Herzogspitalstraße 6, T: (0)89-44 23 23 11

9 **Soul City** Warm and comfy, but not only for the gay community. On Thursdays the club opens its doors to everyone. Then there is plenty of punch for free and lots of hits and oldies. NB: Long queues at the door but the bouncer lets everyone in.
Maximiliansplatz 5, T: (0)89-59 52 72

9 **Soul City** Warm und gemütlich, aber nicht nur für Schwule. Do wird die Disko auch für Heteros geöffnet. Dann gibt's Bowle satt für umsonst, und jede Menge Schlager und Oldies. Achtung: Lange Schlangen. Aber der Türsteher lässt jeden rein.
Maximiliansplatz 5, T: 089-59 52 72

10 **Milchbar** ist ein Feierschuppen vom anderen Stern. Geöffnet bis in die frühen Morgenstunden, wenn die ersten Sonnenstrahlen daran erinnern, dass ein neuer Wiesn-Tag beginnt. In der Woche von 22 bis 6 Uhr und am Wochenende sogar bis 9 Uhr früh geöffnet.
Friedenstraße 10, T: 089-45 02 880

Milchbar

Und noch mehr Ausgehtipps gibt es unter: www.muenchenx.de

Übernachtungen

Meine Favoriten:

1 **Hotel Gästehaus Englischer Garten** Klein, aber fein und familiär mit Traumlage im Grünen. 12 Betten, DZ ab 98,- Euro.
Liebergesellstraße 8, T: 089-38 39 410
www.hotelenglishgarden.de

2 **Hotel Opéra** Mitten in München aufwachen wie in einem Stadtpalais. Jedes Zimmer ist anders dekoriert, mal bayerisch, mal italienisch. 54 Betten, DZ ab 150,- Euro.
St.-Anna-Straße 10, T: 089-22 55 33
www.hotel-opera.de

3 **Hotel Cortiina** Für Feng Shui-Fans. Aber alles andere als kühl. In der Lobby

10 **Milchbar** is a party venue from another planet. Open until the early hours of the morning, when the first rays of sunshine remind you that a new Oktoberfest day begins. On weekdays from 22:00 to 06:00, and at weekends until 09:00 in the morning.
Friedenstraße 10, T: (0)89-45 02 880

More information on Munich's nightlife can be found at: www.muenchenx.de

Accommodation

My favourites (country code ++49):

1 **Hotel Gästehaus Englischer Garten** Quite small, but good with a family atmosphere and a dream location near the park. 12 beds, double room from €98.
Liebergesellstraße 8, T: (0)89-38 39 410
www.hotelenglishgarden.de

2 **Hotel Opéra** Wake up in the centre of Munich like in a manor house. Each room has been decorated in a different style, Bavarian the one, Italian the next. 54 beds, double room from €150.
St.-Anna-Straße 10, T: (0)89-22 55 33
www.hotel-opera.de

Hotel Opéra

3 **Hotel Cortiina** is for fans of Feng Shui. It is everything but cold. In the lobby a cosy open fire crackles. 35 beds, double room from €186.
Ledererstraße 8, T: (0)89-24 22 490
www.cortiina.com

prasselt gemütliches Feuer. 35 Betten, DZ ab 186,- Euro.
Ledererstraße 8, T: 089-24 22 490
www.cortiina.com

4 **Der Bayerische Hof** ist eines der führenden Luxushotels im Herzen Münchens: 395 Traum-Zimmer, Konferenzräume, Restaurants (Trader Vics) und Bars, Pool über den Dächern der Stadt. Zimmer ab 413,- Euro. Tipp: Der Concierge erledigt alles für Sie!
Promenadeplatz 2–6, T: 089-21 200
www.bayerischerhof.de

Bayerischer Hof

5 **Hotel Olympic** ist ein kleines Stadthotel mitten im hippen Gärtnerplatzviertel mit 50 Betten, DZ ab 160,- Euro. Tipp: Das schönste Frühstück gibt's in den Cafes um die Ecke.
Hans-Sachs-Straße 4, T: 089-23 18 90
www.hotel-olympic.de

Mehr Übernachtungstipps im Serviceteil und unter: www.muenchen.de www.ganz-muenchen.de

Vor der Wiesn

Hier gibt es das beste Frühstück:

6 **Cafe Reitschule** ist der Schwabinger Klassiker. Zwar schon leicht patiniert, aber mit seiner Lage direkt am Englischen Garten (Terrasse) und seiner Atmosphäre (Künstler, Studenten) immer noch herrlich liebenswert. Hier schlürfte schon Fürstin Gloria ihren Milchcafe.
Königinstraße 34, T: 089-38 88 760

4 **The Bayerische Hof** hotel is one of the leading luxury hotels in the heart of Munich: 395 dream rooms, conference rooms, restaurants (Trader Vics) and bars, swimming pool above the city's rooftops. Rooms from €413. Tip: Reception will arrange everything for you!
Promenadeplatz 2–6, T: (0)89-21 200
www.bayerischerhof.de

5 **Hotel Olympic** is a small city hotel in the middle of the trendy area around the Gärtnerplatz, with 50 beds, double room from €160. Tip: The best breakfasts are available in the cafes around the corner.
Hans-Sachs-Straße 4, T: (0)89-23 18 90
www.hotel-olympic.de

More accommodation tips in the information section in this guide and at: www.ganz-muenchen.de www.muenchen.de

Before the 'Wiesn'

the best breakfasts are available here:

6 **Cafe Reitschule** is the classic cafe in Munich-Schwabing. Although slightly getting on in years, with its great location right next to the Englischer Garten (terrace) and its atmosphere (artists, students), it is still pleasant and agreeable. Gloria von Thurn and Taxis used to have her cafe-latte here.
Königinstraße 34, T: (0)89-38 88 760

7 **Cafe Roma** is where sunglasses on perfect noses meet. Situated on Munich's luxury shopping street, all those who meet again later in the Käfer tent or the Schützen-Festhalle with a mug of beer in their hands go here for breakfast or lunch.
Maximilianstraße 31, T: (0)89-22 74 35

Cafe Roma

7 **Cafe Roma** ist der Treffpunkt der Sonnenbrillen auf perfekten Nasen. An der feinen Münchner Shoppingmeile trifft sich hier zum Frühstück/Lunch alles, was sich später im Käfer- oder Schützenzelt vor der Maß wieder sieht.
Maximilianstraße 31, T: 089-22 74 35

8 **Dukatz** im Literaturhaus ist très très französisch. Hier küsst Sie morgens der beste Kaffee der Stadt wach.
Salvatorplatz 1, T: 089-29 19 600

9 **Glockenspiel** ist eine windgeschützte Sonnenterrasse im 4. Stock mit Blick aufs Rathaus, auf coole Leute und das berühmte Glockenspiel.
Marienplatz 28, T: 089-26 42 56

Glockenspiel

10 **Zum Franziskaner** ist mindestens ein Einmal-Must vor der Maß: Hier wird Münchens traditionelles Weißwurstfrühstück mit süßem Senf und Brezn serviert.
Residenzstraße 9, Tel: 0 89-23 18 120

Restauranttipps für einen Wiesn-Austag:

11 **Restaurant Schmock** bietet viele Gründe hinzugehen: die koschere Currywurst, die israelischen Vorspeisen, das beste Steak. Die Musik dort ist genauso gut. Es könnte auch in New York sein, ist aber ein angesagter Treffpunkt in München.
Augustenstraße 52, T: 089-52 35 05 35

8 **Dukatz** in the Literaturhaus is très, très français. Here the best coffee in town kisses you awake in the morning.
Salvatorplatz 1, T: (0)89-29 19 600

9 **Glockenspiel** is a sun terrace protected from the wind, on the fourth floor with a view of the town hall, of cool passers-by and of Munich's famous Glockenspiel (chimes).
Marienplatz 28, T: (0)89-26 42 56

10 **The Franziskaner** should be experienced at least once, before you visit the Oktoberfest: Munich's traditional white veal sausage breakfast is served here with sweet mustard and pretzels.
Residenzstraße 9, T: (0)89-23 18 120

Restaurant tips for a day off from the Oktoberfest:

11 **Restaurant Schmock** has many enticing things on offer: the kosher curry-sausage, the Israeli starters, the best steak. The music here is equally good. This could all be in New York, but it is a hip place to be in Munich.
Augustenstraße 52, T: (0)89-52 35 05 35

Restaurant Schmock

12 **Yum** is not a Bavarian restaurant, but Thai. Nevertheless with Munich flair. This is where the glitterati eat. And therefore people are quite happy to queue for a table.
Utzschneiderstraße 6, T: (0)89-23 23 06 60

12 **Yum** ist kein bayerisches Lokal, sondern ein Thailänder. Allerdings mit münchnerischen Allüren. Hier tafelt die Szene, darum wartet man gern mal auf einen Tisch.
Utzschneiderstraße 6, T: 089-23 23 06 60

13 **Schumanns Tagesbar** ist mittags der Stammtisch der Eliten (Mode, Medien) und Eitelkeiten (Zahnärzte, Anwälte), die sich zu deftiger Kost (Pellkartoffeln mit Quark) treffen. Und sich abends ein paar Türen weiter im Schumanns in der Ludwigstraße ganz gebauchpinselt fühlen, wenn Chef Charles Schumann an ihren Tisch kommt.
Maffeistraße 6, T: 089-24 21 77 00

Schumanns Tagesbar

14 **Trader Vics** Keine Lust mehr auf Hendl oder Ochsen? Hier gibt es die besten Spare-Rips und tausend thailändische Köstlichkeiten. Fragen Sie nach Herrn Hew (Reservierungschef) und einem „Zombi" (k.o.-Drink) und der Abend wird ein Knüller.
Hotel Bayerischer Hof,
Promenadeplatz 2–6, T: 089-21 20 995

15 **Käfer-Schänke** ist ein Münchner Gourmet-Klassiker. Ur-gemütlich sitzt man in kleinen Stübchen und genießt bayerisch-mediterrane Küche, z.B. Tartar mit Kartoffelschnee und Kaviar. Und irgendwo sitzt immer ein Prominenter!
Prinzregentenstaße 73, T: 089-41 68 247

16 **Brenner** ist mittags ein Renner. Weil es ein wunderschönes Ambiente hat, dazu hübsch gekleidete Menschen, und der lauwarme Gemüsesalat ein Gedicht ist.
Maximilianstraße 15, T: 089-45 22 880

13 **Schumanns Tagesbar** is the regular place where the elite (fashion, media) and the vain (dentists, lawyers) meet for lunch: Good decent food (jacket potatoes with white cream cheese). In the evenings they go only a few doors down the road to Schumann's in Ludwigstraße and feel quite flattered when Chef Charles Schumann comes to their table.
Maffeistraße 6, T: (0)89-24 21 77 00

14 **Trader Vics** Fed up with chicken or ox? Here you will find the best spare ribs and a thousand Thai delicacies. Ask for Mr. Hew (reservations manager) and a 'Zombi' (a knock out drink) and the evening will be a hit.
Hotel Bayerischer Hof,
Promenadeplatz 2–6, T: (0)89-21 20 995

15 **Käfer-Schänke** is a Munich gourmet classic. One sits in small, very cosy, screened-off areas and enjoys Bavarian-Mediterranean cuisine. For example tartar with potato mash and caviar, and somewhere there will always be a celebrity sitting nearby!
Prinzregentenstraße 73, T: (0)89-41 68 247

Käfer-Schänke

16 **Brenner** is a real hit at lunchtime because it has such a wonderful atmosphere, including well-dressed people, and the warm vegetable salad is simply divine.
Maximilianstraße 15, T: (0)89-45 22 880

Serviceteil

Sie brauchen unbedingt ein Aspirin gegen Schädelbrummen? Ihr Schlüssel ist weg, obschon Sie im Dekollete Ihrer Nachbarin alles abgesucht haben? Sie wissen nicht wohin mit ihrem sperrigen Kinderwagen? Und überhaupt: Wie erreichen Sie das Oktoberfest am besten – zu Fuß, per Bus, im Taxi?
Unser „Service-Kapitel" hat die Antworten auf alle Fragen.
Die wichtigsten Informationen und Telefonnummern:

Auf zur Wiesn mit den Öffentlichen – alle Linien im Überblick:

♦ **S-Bahn:**
S1 bis S8 zur Hackerbrücke, von dort zu Fuß auf die Theresienwiese

S7 und S27 bis Heimeranplatz, weiter mit U4 oder U5 auf die Wiesn

♦ **U-Bahn:**
U3 oder U6, Zielbahnhöfe Goetheplatz und Poccistraße, von dort zu Fuß

U4 oder U5 bis Theresienwiese oder Schwanthaler Höhe (direkt am Ziel)

♦ **Straßenbahn:**
Linie 18 (bis Haltestelle Hermann-Lingg-Straße)

Linie 19 (bis Haltestelle Hermann-Lingg-Straße)

♦ **Bus:**
Linie 31 (Haltestelle Hans-Fischer-Straße oder Poccistraße)

Linie 58 (Haltestelle Goetheplatz)

Linie 66 (Haltestellen Alter Messeplatz, Theresienhöhe oder Hans-Fischer-Straße)

General information and services

You have an urgent need for an Aspirin to ease the throbbing pain in your head? And you cannot find your key, although you've already had a good look around in the cleavage of your lady friend? You don't know what to do with the bulky pram? But, in any case: What's the best way to get to the Oktoberfest ... on foot, by bus, in a taxi? Our services information chapter has the answer to all your questions and includes the most important information and phone numbers:

Travelling to the Oktoberfest by public transport–All lines and routes at one glance:

♦ **Suburban trains (S-Bahn):**
S1 through S8: to Hackerbrücke, then a short walk to Theresienwiese (Oktoberfest park, follow signs)

S7 and S27: to Heimeranplatz, then with U4 or U5 to Theresienwiese (Oktoberfest park)

♦ **Underground trains (U-Bahn):**
U3 or U6, stop Goetheplatz or Poccistraße, then a short walk

U4 or U5 to Theresienwiese or Schwanthaler Höhe (stops closest to the Oktoberfest)

♦ **Tramway:**
Route 18 (to tram stop: Hermann-Lingg-Straße)

Route 19 (to tram stop: Hermann-Lingg-Straße)

♦ **Bus:**
No. 31 (bus stop Hans-Fischer-Straße or Poccistraße)

No. 58 (bus stop Goetheplatz)

No. 66 (bus stop Alter Messeplatz, Theresienhöhe or Hans-Fischer-Straße)

Wann hat das Oktoberfest geöffnet?

♦ **Bierausschank**
Wochentags: 10 bis 22:30 Uhr
Samstags, Sonn- und feiertags: 9 bis 22:30 Uhr

♦ **Tägliche Schlussstunde in den Zelten:** 23:30 Uhr
Käfer's Wies'n Schänke und das Weinzelt haben bis 1 Uhr geöffnet. Ende des Ausschanks dort: 0:15 Uhr.

♦ **Schausteller:**
Montag bis Donnerstag: 10 bis 23:30 Uhr
Freitag, Samstag: 10 bis 24 Uhr
Sonn- und feiertags: 10 bis 23:30 Uhr

♦ **Familientage:**
Dienstage (12 Uhr bis 18 Uhr) sind in jedem Jahr die Familientage. Ermäßigte Fahr-, Eintritts- und Verkaufspreise!

Alle Telefonnummern rund um das Oktoberfest:

(Landesvorwahl: ++49-(0) 89-...)

Taxi:

♦ Taxizentrale München, T: 089-21 61 0

♦ Jumbo Taxi (Großraumtaxi bis sieben Pers.), T: 089-74 57 65 77

♦ Sechs Taxistände rund ums Oktoberfest sorgen für genügend Nachschub.
Tipp: Bestellen Sie sich für den spätnächtlichen Heimweg, wenn alle Zelte schließen, ein Taxi an einen bestimmten Treffpunkt vor.

Hilfe:

♦ Bayerisches Rotes Kreuz Notruf, T: 089-50 22 22 22

♦ Fundbüro (Oktoberfest), T: 089-23 33 02 98

♦ Wiesn-Polizei, T: 089-500 32 20

What are the opening hours?

♦ **Serving beer:**
Weekdays: 10:00 to 22:30
Saturdays, Sundays and public holidays: 09:00 to 22:30

♦ **Beer tents close every day at:** 23:30
Käfer's Wies'n Schänke and the Weinzelt (wine tent) are open until 01:00 am. Last orders are at 00:15 am.

♦ **Fairground attractions:**
Monday to Thursday: 10:00 – 23:30
Fridays, Saturdays: 10:00 – 00:00
Sundays and public holidays: 10:00 – 23:30

♦ **Family days:**
Tuesdays (12:00 – 18:00) are the family days every year.
On these days prices are generally reduced across the Oktoberfest.

All phone numbers relating to the Oktoberfest:

International dialling code for Germany ++49–then for Munich (0) 89 - ...

Taxi:

♦ Munich's taxi centre (Taxizentrale München), T: (0)89-21 61 0

♦ Jumbo Taxi (up to seven passengers), T: (0)89-74 57 65 77

♦ Six taxi ranks around the Oktoberfest ensure a smooth service.
Tip: Book your taxi in advance for your night-time trip home, when all the beer tents close, arrange for the taxi to pick you up at a specific meeting point.

Help and emergency:

♦ Emergency phone: Bavarian Red Cross (Bayerisches Rotes Kreuz), T: (0)89-50 22 22 22

♦ Lost property (Oktoberfest), T: (0)89-23 33 02 98

♦ Oktoberfest police department (Polizei), T: (0)89-500 32 20

Auskunft und Informationen:

♦ Festleitung und Information zum Oktoberfest, T: 089-23 33 02 91

♦ Tourismus-Information (Tourismusamt), T: 089-2 33 96 500

♦ Flugauskunft Flughafen München, T: 089-97 52 13 13

♦ MVV (Münchener Verkehrsverbund), T: 089-21 03 30

♦ Wiesn-Führungen, T: 089-23 23 900

♦ Stadtführungen, T: 089-2 33 30-231 oder -234

Die Internetseiten zum Oktoberfest:

www.oktoberfest.de
www.festring-muenchen.de
www.ganz-muenchen.de
www.oktoberfest-tv.de
www.oktoberfest2005.de
www.muenchen-tourist.de

Allgemeine Infos für Übernachtungen:

Hotels:

♦ Münchner Hotel Verbund GmbH
T: 01805-30 77 50
Website: **www.muenchen-hotel.de**
Hier gilt natürlich: Zur Wiesn-Zeit ist es sehr schwer, in München ein Zimmer zu bekommen. Darum unbedingt früh buchen.

♦ Die STATTHOTEL OHG ist eine Service-Agentur, die sich auf die Vermittlung von individuellen Wohnmöglichkeiten in und um München spezialisiert hat.
T: 0180-5 30 55 30
Weitere Informationen im Internet unter **www.statthotel.de**

♦ Der Fremdenverkehrsverein bietet ein Hotel- und Pensionsverzeichnis im Internet: **www.muenchen-tourist.de**

Information:

♦ Oktoberfest management and information, T: (0)89-23 33 02 91

♦ Tourist information (Munich tourist office), T: (0)89-2 33 96 500

♦ Flight information at Munich airport, T: (0)89-97 52 13 13

♦ Transport information: Munich public transport (MVV), T: (0)89-21 03 30

♦ Oktoberfest guided tours, T: (0)89-23 23 900

♦ Guided city tours, T: (0)89-2 33 30-231 or -234

Internet web sites relating to the Oktoberfest:
www.oktoberfest.de
www.festring-muenchen.de
www.ganz-muenchen.de
www.oktoberfest-tv.de
www.oktoberfest2005.de
www.muenchen-tourist.de

General information for accommodation:

Hotels:

♦ Munich hotel association (Münchner Hotel Verbund GmbH)
T: (++49)(0)1805-30 77 50
Website: **www.muenchen-hotel.de**
It is important to remember that during the Oktoberfest period it is very difficult to find accommodation in Munich. It is therefore necessary to book early.

♦ STATTHOTEL OHG is an agency specializing in allocation of private accommodation in and around Munich.
T: (++49)(0)180-5 30 55 30
Further information online, at **www.statthotel.de**.

♦ The tourism association (Fremdenverkehrsverein) offers information on hotel and guest houses online at: **www.muenchen-tourist.de**

Unter **www.oktoberfest-reservierung.de** und **www.oktoberfest-info.com** findet der Besucher einen Reservierungsservice sowohl für Hotelzimmer, als auch für Festzelte auf der Wiesn.

♦ Gemütlich in möblierten Appartements: Nutzen Sie die preiswerten Übernachtungskonditionen: Infos unter **www.stay-munich.de**

Camping:

Per Wohnmobil: Es ist nicht erlaubt, während der Wiesnzeit mit einem Wohnmobil im Stadtbereich zu übernachten.

♦ Fremdenverkehrsamt München, Tel.-Zentrale, T: 089-23 30 300

♦ Campingplatz Obermenzing, T: 089-8 11 22 35

♦ Campingplatz Thalkirchen, T: 089-7 23 17 07

Mit dem Rollstuhl ins Bierzelt

Als Rollstuhlfahrer auf das größte Volksfest der Welt? Kein Problem. Wenn man weiß, welche speziellen Einrichtungen es gibt, und man ein paar Dinge beachtet. So haben z.B. alle Bierzelte und Festbetriebe Zugänge von außen, die entweder ebenerdig oder mit Rampen versehen sind. Genaue Infos unter: **www.wiesnhandi.de**

Die Wiesntermine für die kommenden fünf Jahre:

2005: 17. September bis 3. Oktober (verlängert wegen Feiertag)
2006: 16. September bis 3. Oktober (verlängert wegen Feiertag)
2007: 22. September bis 7. Oktober
2008: 20. September bis 5. Oktober
2009: 19. September bis 4. Oktober

At **www.oktoberfest-reservierung.de** and **www.oktoberfest-info.com** you will find a reservation service for hotel rooms as well as for tables/seating at beer tents at the Oktoberfest.

♦ Comfort in furnished apartments: Make use of reasonably priced accommodation: Information at **www.stay-munich.de**

Camping:

In caravans: It is not permitted to sleep overnight in a caravan within the city limits during the Oktoberfest.

♦ Munich tourist office (central office), T: (0)89-23 30 300

♦ Campingplatz Obermenzing (camping site), T: (0)89-8 11 22 35

♦ Campingplatz Thalkirchen (camping site), T: (0)89-7 23 17 07

Disabled access to the beer tents

In a wheelchair at the world's greatest beer festival? No problem, if you know which arrangements have been made and if you take a few things into consideration. For example, all beer tents and fairground attractions have access points which are either at ground level or fitted with a ramp. More information at: **www.wiesnhandi.de**

Oktoberfest dates for the next five years:

2005: 17 September to 3 October (extended due to public holiday)
2006: 16 September to 3 October (extended due to public holiday)
2007: 22 September to 7 October
2008: 20 September to 5 October
2009: 19 September to 4 October